RETHINKING STRATEGIC COMPENSATION

2ND EDITION

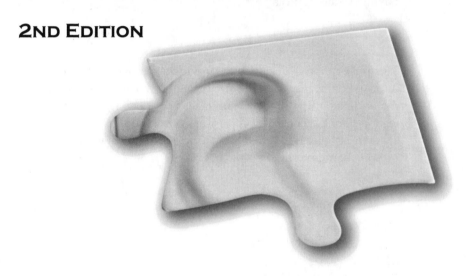

BRENT M. LONGNECKER, CCP, CBP, CCC

CCH INCORPORATED
Chicago

A WoltersKluwer Company

Publisher: Robert Becker

Production Coordinator: Rebekah J. Grubisic
                        Lauren Miller

Cover Design: Erika Dix, Laila Gaidulis

Interior Design: Erika Dix

Layout: Craig Arritola

ISBN 0-8080-1367-X
©2005 CCH INCORPORATED
4025 W. Peterson Ave.
Chicago, IL 60646-6085
1 800 248 3248
hr.cch.com

A WoltersKluwer Company

ACKNOWLEDGEMENTS

This book is dedicated to all the great professionals across the world who work each and every day trying to attract, retain and motivate the most important asset any company has – its people. Typically overworked and under appreciated, their contribution to commerce is the single most important contribution imaginable.

This book could not have been written without the help of dozens of people. I particularly want to extend thanks to the following individuals and companies who contributed mightily to this project: Chris Crawford, April Canik, Tammy Hemphill, Sharon Cross, Brice Simpson, Nathan White, Josh Henke, Shane Krantz and Malcolm Dorman. Thanks also to WorldatWork and Anne Ruddy's great group who were always there to answer our questions. And a special thanks to Teri Longnecker, Jennifer Sprauer, Alena Aicklen and Adrian Quintana who were all responsible for making sure that ideas got down on paper. To each and every one of these people—I am grateful.

To **CCH** INCORPORATED, I say "thanks" for allowing me to write on a subject that I am passionate about. In addition, I appreciate your guidance, edits and encouragement throughout. Any errors are mine. I had a great team undertake a considerable amount of research that we simply could not include in the print version of this book.

BIOGRAPHY

Author Brent M. Longnecker, CCP, CBP, CCC, is president of Long-necker & Associates, Inc., (longneckerandassociates.com) and a leading expert is strategic compensation, corporate governance and human resource planning. He has more than 20 years of experience in the analysis, design and implementation of innovative performance and productivity-enhancement programs. Longnecker also has been selected as one of the Top 25 Most Influential Consultants 2005 in the United States by *Consulting Magazine*–the first in the field of executive pay. His consulting engagements with compensation committees, attorneys, executives and others, in all industries, have embraced and dealt with a myriad of issues ranging from analysis to expert testimony; from incentive plan design to the design of compensation committee charters. He has authored over 200 articles and seven books.

Prior to forming Longnecker & Associates, Longnecker was president of Resources Consulting group, a spin-off of Deloitte & Touche where he served as national Partner-in-charge of Deloitte's performance management and compensation consulting practice.

Contents

CHAPTER TWO

CHAPTER THREE

CHAPTER FOUR

CHAPTER FIVE

Chapter Six

Rewarding employees and managing the bottom line   **121**

Chapter Seven

When the best should earn the most   **135**

Chapter Eight

Taking care of the executive team   **145**

Index   **157**

CHAPTER ONE

BASE, VARIABLE AND PERFORMANCE-BASED COMPENSATION

OBJECTIVES

In today's corporate or business world, the competition for top talent is fiercer than ever. One of the primary fields of battle for top talent is the area of compensation. In order to compete and win in this area, companies must build and implement successful compensation strategies and reward systems.

KEY POINTS

◊ Base salary, short-term incentives, long-term incentives, benefits, and perquisites work in concert to provide the organization with an abundant supply of motivated employees.
◊ Corporate culture and organizational strategies must be aligned.
◊ The ability to effectively design multiple compensation strategies is key to the harmonization of strategy and culture.

Before exploring every nook and cranny of compensation, business leaders should first review corporate strategy and organizational design. Compensation is only a piece, although an important one, of the total organizational structure. Without a defined corporate strategy, compensation plans run a high risk of being unsuccessful.

The direction and intent of the company should be clear, focused and well communicated. If ambiguous, the person or team designing the compensation package should discuss and get consensus on the direction of the company with the company's decision makers (board of directors, owner, CEO, etc.) as a first step

The strategy of the organization is important because it greatly affects how the company is structured. Likewise, the design of the organization is important insofar as it supports the strategy.

> *Generally, management of a large force is the same as the management of a few men: it is a matter of organization. And to direct a large army to fight is the same as to direct a small one: it is a matter of command signs and signals.*
>
> —Sun Tzu

BEST PRACTICE

The Star model. A popular way of viewing the structure of an organization is the Star model attributed to Jay R. Galbraith. In this model, five areas are used to describe the characteristics of the organizational design. These five areas are:

- **Strategy**—an organized set of goals and vision which capitalize on those areas that are deemed core competencies by the organizational leadership.

- **Structure**—the formal roles of people in an organization. Structure involves concepts such as power distance (which is the extent to which less powerful employees accept that power is – and should be – distributed unequally) and chain of command.

- **Processes**—the actual method by which things get done. Typically, processes are viewed in macro terms as either top-down (resource allocation) or between departments (product development).

- **People**—the policies of the firm that relate to the procurement and development of talent in an organization.

- **Rewards**—a system that encourages employees to act in a manner that is consistent with the corporate strategy.

To these five parts of the Star model, some organizations also add an element which encompasses the entire star: culture. In order for a business organization to be successful, all elements of the organizational design must be in alignment. Corporate culture is seen as the glue that keeps the parts of the star aligned with each other through the employees' shared sets of values and experiences.

Because compensation is part of the toolset that adds vitality to the organizational design, the actual structure of the organization is important to the development of a compensation package. Compensation is a key piece of the People and Rewards elements of the Star model. Because of the way compensation is used to influence the types of people drawn to an organization, it is an important factor in corporate culture as well.

Once the organizational design is aligned with the strategy, the acquisition of talented employees that fit organizational needs becomes essential. Compensation is one of the primary means of attracting the right people. Once hired, employees need to be rewarded for their performance and productivity. Again, a well-designed compensation plan can provide this direction and incentive for employees.

DEFINITION

Compensation for the employee is defined by WorldatWork as the total sum (both extrinsic and intrinsic) economic benefit received by the employee in return for services rendered to the employer. For the employer, compensation can be defined as the cost of providing those economic benefits to the employee. This book will examine compensation from both the employee's and the employer's perspectives.

Compensation is critical because it is the primary means of attracting, retaining, and motivating talented employees. Of course, each piece of a compensation package plays a different role in contributing to the attraction, retention, and/or motivation. A discussion of these elements will be presented later in this chapter.

Typically, a discussion of compensation packages is centered around compensation for highly-compensated executives. Although some discussion of compensation for specific groups of employees will take place, most of this book will focus on executive and key employee compensation packages.

The definition of executive is somewhat nebulous. Different companies define the term differently, and some do not make a distinction between executives and other employees at all. Often, executives can be identified by title. Corporate officers are almost always considered executives. However, the best way of describing an executive is *anyone who has significant impact on the results of the enterprise.*

The groups of employees that will be discussed in this book come from a range of functions. These functions include hourly manual labor, middle management and, increasingly, "knowledge workers." Because the knowledge worker group is growing the fastest, most of the discussion that does not focus on executives will focus on this increasingly important category.

THE TOTAL COMPENSATION PACKAGE

The total compensation package builds off of the business strategy and serves as the roadmap to success in the building of reward packages. Further, WorldatWork teaches that there is a circular process that completes the total rewards cycle. (Figure 1: Total Rewards Cycle). It shows that any program designed needs to be in sync with both the mission and business strategies of the organization. The obstacle is to drive desired behaviors into a workforce that will enhance the chances of organizational success.

As stated previously, companies must have a well-designed compensation plan in order to attract, retain, and motivate talented employees. What is a compensation plan? A compensation plan should be viewed as the *total compensation package*. This approach is important because compensation is made up of several elements, which must work in tandem to meet all of the goals of the compensation plan. Taken individually, none of these elements are capable of

Figure 1-1. *Total Rewards Design Process*

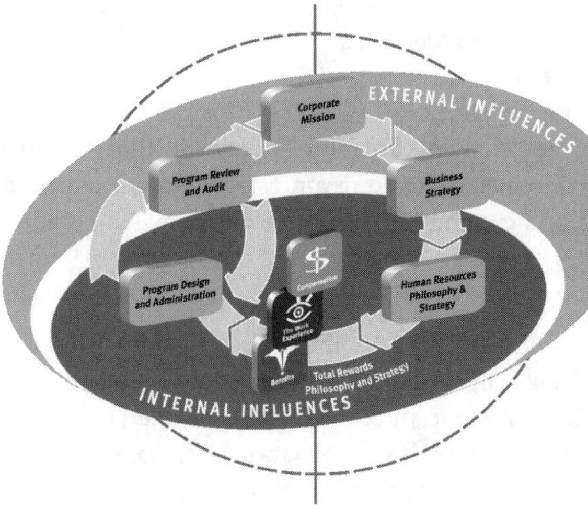

Source: WorldAtWork

providing the means to completely achieve the goals of attracting, retaining, and/or motivating any qualified employee.

Employees view the total compensation package as a way to achieve a variety of personal goals. The package can provide a means to achieve a lifestyle, to accumulate wealth, to ensure security, and to boost self-esteem. By permitting the employee to achieve these objectives, the compensation package becomes a highly effective method of inspiring the employee to focus on the work ahead of them.

Employers tend to view the total compensation package as a cost or at best – an investment. They try to balance the package in a way that achieves the biggest impact with the employee for the least amount of actual cost. As well as a cost, total compensation can be viewed as a competitive advantage for employers. A well-designed package will allow companies to attract and retain talent that will provide them with a competitive edge. The proper package design will also give employees the incentive to reach higher levels of productivity than otherwise attainable.

What are the elements of a total compensation system? A total compensation package has five key elements. These elements are:
- Base salary
- Short-term incentives
- Long-term incentives
- Benefits
- Perquisites

Some elements are more effective in attracting new talent. Others provide incentives to retain existing talent with the company. The remaining elements help to motivate existing talent.

BASE SALARY

Base salary is typically the cornerstone piece of any compensation package. This is usually the key piece in the average compensation package. As employees reach more exalted ranks, the impact of base salary on the total compensation package is lessened.

Base salary in the United States has been impacted by several federal regulations:
- The Fair Labor Standards Act of 1938;
- The Equal Pay Act of 1963;
- Title VII of the Civil Rights Act of 1964; and
- The Age Discrimination in Employment Act of 1967.

The Fair Labor Standards Act

The *Fair Labor Standards Act (FLSA)* was passed in an effort to guarantee a minimum living standard for industrial workers and to curb abusive employment practices. The need for this type of legislation was publicized by the efforts of labor unions in the early part of the twentieth century. The FLSA made employers more responsible for treating workers fairly. Through wage guidelines, this legislation sets baselines for the salary portion of the total compensation package.

Minimum wage laws originated with this legislation. The minimum wage is the pay rate that organizations must guarantee their employees. This guaranteed minimum pay rate is a requirement regardless of the basis for pay. Pay must be distributed on an hourly, piece, or hourly-plus-tips basis. In all of these situations, the employee is entitled to a wage rate equivalent to the federal minimum wage set by Congress.

Another important concept relating to base salary introduced in the FLSA is that of exemption. The FLSA contains guidelines to differentiate between types of positions. These distinctions, which have become fuzzy in today's employment environment, are exempt and nonexempt.

DEFINITION

Exempt employees are typically in supervisory and professional positions and above.

Nonexempt employees are usually line employees such as assembly line workers or construction laborers.

The primary difference between these two classifications relates to the structure of the base salary. Exempt employees are paid a salary that is not dependent on actual hours worked. Nonexempt employees are paid hourly, piece rate, or some other wage rate directly related to the amount of work performed. The most important difference between the exempt and nonexempt categories is that exempt workers are not paid overtime.

The FLSA also includes provisions and guidelines for overtime pay. These provisions include a bump in pay rate for any time worked in excess of 40 hours per week. The pay rate for time in excess of 40 hours is one-and-a-half times the base pay rate. An important consideration to overtime pay is the impact of nondiscretionary bonuses. Even though nondiscretionary bonuses, which will be discussed in later sections, are not considered part of the base salary, they are included in the calculation of the base pay rate used to determine overtime pay.

The next three pieces of legislation—all from the 1960s—that impact base salary primarily target discriminatory, practices. During much of the history of the United States, hiring and pay practices were disparate, discriminatory, or inequitable. Typically, males of Northern European (but not Irish) descent were hired first and paid more than others. As the civil rights movements of the 1960s brought a level of public attention to the discriminatory employment practices of businesses, Congress enacted legislation in an effort to end the disparity in opportunities and pay.

The Equal Pay Act

The *Equal Pay Act (EPA)* was intended to end the disparity of pay between men and women. The EPA prohibits unequal pay for the same work. The legislation also sets guidelines to use when defining equal work. The guidelines are as follows:

- **Skill**—experience, training, education, and abilities
- **Effort**—either physical or mental
- **Responsibility**—degree of accountability
- **Working conditions**—temperature, height, hazards, etc.

Despite these guidelines, the term "equal work" is still subject to much interpretation. Over the last 40 years, the intent of the EPA has not completely materialized. However, pay situations for females have improved relative to males.

BEST PRACTICE

A cure for "water cooler" chatter

Company name:	**EPM, Inc.**
Problem faced by company:	EPM, Inc. was beginning to have problems with employees who served as supervisors and managers for their company's largest product line. The employees, through "water-cooler" talk, found that some of them were being paid a straight salary with no bonus, some were being paid hourly with compensation for overtime, and some were being paid salary with bonus. The company realized that their current pay practices were jeopardizing their ability to retain employees and putting the company at risk for lawsuits and other labor violations.
Compensation solutions:	The first task was to create job descriptions for both positions in question. Once the actual job duties were outlined, a review was done based on the guidelines presented under FLSA to determine exemption status. A comprehensive compensation review was then conducted to determine market competitive base salary and bonus levels. The exemption status was made uniform for all employees in both positions. The ultimate decision was that both positions were exempt; therefore, the company (armed with the market compensation data) created salary ranges for the two positions. Individuals were placed within the ranged based on their individual experience and past performance.
Benefit to company:	The company ensured that compensation practices would be uniform within each specific job, which then led to greater retention of employees and higher morale.

Title VII of the Civil Rights Act

Title VII of the Civil Rights Act prohibits employment discrimination based on race, color, religion, sex, or national origin. This legislation is intended to provide opportunity in employment for anyone despite any differences in appearance or beliefs. Title VII governs all aspects of the employment process including hiring, firing, compensation, and benefits. The impact of Title VII on the compensation package is one of compliance. Companies must check the impact of compensation packages to verify that they meet the requirements, even if no intent to discriminate against any group or individual exists.

Age Discrimination in Employment Act

The *Age Discrimination in Employment Act* expanded the basis of proscribed discrimination to include age. This legislation specifically states that employers are prohibited from discriminating against employees or job applicants who are age 40 or over. The guidelines and the impact of this legislation are much the same as those of Title VII.

Other legislative initiatives limiting workplace discrimination are the *Vocational Rehabilitation Act* and *The Americans With Disabilities Act,* which ensure workplace rights for those with disabilities.

BASE SALARY

EMPLOYEE VIEW OF BASE SALARY

For employees, the base salary is the primary means of supporting their lifestyle. It provides a minimum expectation of income for the employee in return for his or her efforts on behalf of the employer.

DEFINITION

The base salary is a regular source of income that is used to service the typical expenses that the employee may incur. These expenses include such basic needs as housing, food, clothing, and transportation. Obviously, different people view their basic needs differently and, therefore, will have different base salary requirements.

Depending on the value an individual places on savings and budgets, the base salary can become a source of wealth. In order for this to happen, though, the individual must place a priority on savings and investing and have the discipline to follow a plan. Unfortunately, many in the United States do not find a way to use their salaries to generate future wealth.

Salary also has a psychological value for employees. The base salary is often the most straightforward element of compensation and lends itself well to comparison. Many people make decisions on job offers based on salary because it carries the most guarantees and is easy to compare among competing opportunities. Whenever neighbors discuss compensation, they are usually comparing their base salaries.

As individuals progress up the hierarchy of organizations, base salary decreases in importance to them. In part, this decrease is because employees in higher organizational positions have different expectations of their compensation packages. These individuals typically do not receive as much marginal benefit from an increase in base salary as those at a lower pay scale. The primary reason for the decrease in marginal benefit is the impact of income taxes. Any additional income paid to someone with an already high income is taxed at a higher rate than additional income for someone whose income is substantially less. Executives also have different expectations of the compensation package because they typically have a better understanding of the inter-related pieces of the total compensation package.

EMPLOYER VIEW OF BASE SALARY

The biggest difference between how employees and employers view base salary revolves around the fact that employees see base salary as an income and employers see it as an expense. Depending on the nature of the position, a base salary may be viewed as a variable cost or a fixed cost. Typically, wages related to nonexempt positions (particularly those in the manufacturing, services billed by the hour, and construction sectors) are recorded as variable costs that are actually tied to production. Exempt jobs, on the other hand, are usually considered fixed expenses that are assigned to overhead.

Another role of base salary in the employer's view of the total compensation package is to set baselines. The base salary typically has both a minimum and maximum rate that the company is willing to pay for a job. A base salary also serves as a binding retainer for the services of a particular employee.

Base salaries are the most straightforward and transparent elements of a total compensation package. They serve as a starting point for the construction of any compensation package. Because base salary is the most visible and understandable piece of the total compensation package, it is extremely important in the attraction of talent. Until recently, it has been the most regulated part of the compensation package.

SHORT-TERM INCENTIVES

Short-term incentives are also referred to as bonuses, annual incentives, or variable pay. These incentives are typically tied to achieving certain performance targets set for the company or the individual. Some important differences exist between the types of short-term incentives. Those differences include participant eligibility, individual versus group performance, metrics used to determine the payout, discretionary factors, and the form of payout (cash, equity, etc.).

Variable pay

Variable pay is usually defined in an agreement, the employment letter, or contract. These incentives are often called "at-risk pay" because they place the onus on the employee to perform. This works off the concept of expectancy. Variable pay is derived several different ways. Usually, this incentive is connected to specific job performance.

METRICS

The metrics for determining the amount of variable pay differs, depending on the job function and job level within the organization. The metrics are important components of the design of any compensation package. Metrics and rewards that are aligned with the entire organizational design will encourage employee behavior to support the strategy of the organization.

Some common methods of deriving variable pay are:

- **Commission**—is based on actual effort to generate sales, usually in the form of a percentage of either revenue or profit directly attributable to a particular individual. This incentive is very commonly used with sales personnel.
- **Individual performance**—is associated with the actual performance of the individual as measured against the goals defined and communicated by the organization.
- **Group performance**—is similar in structure to individual performance incentives except the measured performance is based on the group or team.
- **Profit sharing**—is based on the performance of the entire organization. This method typically will involve the entire labor force of the company in order to align workers with the "big picture" of the company.
- **Performance sharing**—typically consolidates several metrics, quantitative and qualitative, used to determine overall company performance in order to determine the payout for each employee. Typical metrics include financial performance, customer satisfaction, and business process, among others. Like profit sharing, this incentive aligns employees with the "big picture," but the criteria are broader.
- **Bonus**—is a variable payment that is not linked to any specific goals – typically very discretionary or subjective. Bonuses come in two varieties, annual (planning cycle) or spot. An annual bonus is usually given as reward for making an outstanding contribution to corporate success. Spot bonuses tend to be smaller and more immediate to recognize a contribution beyond what was necessary over a short amount of time.

Other forms of variable pay exist, but they are more appropriately considered to be long-term incentives. Most variable pay is disbursed on a well-communicated timeline. The timing of disbursement is often annual, depending on the needs of the organization.

Short-term incentives can be linked in a variety of ways, and a company is not restricted to just one type of incentive. It is common for a short-term incentive plan to be allocated between individual, group/team, and organization-wide metrics to determine the amount of the incentive. The weight of each metric on the total size of variable pay usually depends on the employee's level of responsibility.

EMPLOYEE VIEW OF SHORT-TERM INCENTIVES

Short-term incentives are often considered by employees as an extension of their base pay. This perspective is especially true if the achievement targets are not too difficult to reach or if payouts are extremely short, like monthly. The payouts of these incentives are used to supplement the lifestyle supported by the base salary.

Short-term incentives can be used to build wealth. In the United States, they are used more often to buy something outside the normal budget. Boats, large appliances, vacations, home entertainment systems, and computers are often financed by short-term incentives.

Employees can also adopt a negative opinion of short-term incentives. Sometimes the performance targets are set at a level that the employee deems unreachable leading to demoralization and lower productivity. Even worse, the employee can view the incentive payout as an entitlement and borrow against the future income. If the payout is not repeated (due to failure to meet targets, etc.), then the employee may confront financial hardships.

EMPLOYER VIEW OF SHORT-TERM INCENTIVES

Employers view short-term incentives as the carrot held out in front of their employees. Short-term incentives are used by employers to encourage certain behavior by their employees. A well-designed, short-term incentive program will motivate the employee to perform in a manner that aligns performance with the execution of corporate strategy. Companies are constantly attempting to find a mix of appropriate incentives that will encourage employees to achieve maximum performance goals and higher levels of productivity.

Organizations can also view short-term incentive plans with skepticism. This is often the case when the performance hurdles are set too low and employees begin to view the payout as an entitlement. At this point, the incentive element becomes part of the base salary paid in lump sum. (On the bright side, this may be a tax advantage).

METRICS

The metrics used to measure progress toward the incentive targets must be in line with the end goals of the corporation. Companies can also find that short-term incentive plans do not encourage the behaviors that they desire. This occurrence is typically the result of a metric misalignment.

Ultimately, short-term incentives can be a very powerful motivating tool; however, they can also be a double-edged sword. The potential of short-term incentives to guide employees both toward and away from corporate goals requires planners to use great care and thought when designing incentive plans.

BEST PRACTICE

Tying incentives to performance

Company Name:	**LCC Enterprise**
Problem faced by company:	LCC Enterprise was experiencing high turnover and low performance from employees. Upon review of the problem, LCC realized that workers had no idea how they earned incentive (bonus) awards. In fact, many workers did not know a slight increase in productivity would provide them with significant monetary rewards.
Compensation solutions:	A design team was developed, which included managers from all company locations. Each individual was educated on the process of incentive programs so they would have a basic understanding of incentives and how they were created and administered. Market data was collected surrounding target award levels. With this information, the design team determined what type of plan they wanted from a funding perspective and the degree of employee participation. To allocate the funding, they designed both team and individual performance metrics that would determine the actual dollar value that an individual would have earned. This plan design ultimately encompassed everyone from executives through line level employees.
	A focus group was created from a random group of employees to obtain feedback. The plan was tweaked based on their feedback. Finally, a communication document was created to be distributed to all employees.

Benefit to company:	The incentive plan was a success. Employees understood their link between their personal performance, the company's performance, and how they would be rewarded. The company communicated the status of the plan on a monthly basis thus making it easier for the employees to track their performance. The plan has helped reduce turnover and increase individual performance.

LONG-TERM INCENTIVES

Due to recent corporate scandals and perceptions of pay inequities, long-term incentives have entered the "media circus" in headline stories about high profile executives.

DEFINITION

Long-term incentives are those incentives that do not vest during the next year and, in fact, typically do not vest for three to five years. These incentives have typically been equity based. Usually, long-term incentives are awarded as a result of service over time.

As a result of rewarding performance over time, long-term incentives serve to retain talent. The typical application of these incentives is to stagger the vesting time in a manner that requires a departing employee to lose his or her rights to payouts of equity or cash that may have already been promised.

Equity incentives foster employee commitment to the company. Equity incentives may include the following varieties:

- **Stock options**—the right to purchase stock at previously specified prices during a certain time frame after employment requirements are met.
- **Stock grants**—stock given to employees at no cost.
- **Restricted stock**—stock given to employees with the requirement to keep the stock for a given amount of time.
- **Shadow/Phantom stock**—a stock-like device used to allow an employee to profit from stock performance without diluting the ownership of the company. Often these are used by companies that are not publicly held.

The usage of these instruments has been questioned by the media, investors, and others. As a result of several recent abuses and many suspected abuses, these instruments are under increased scrutiny. Despite the negative perception of these instruments, long-term incentives provide a potent method of retaining talent and aligning management-level employees with the goals and objectives of the company.

> *Options have become the drug of choice used to keep existing talent and seduce the bright young stars of the future...Options packages became the scorecard for the executive team.*
> —Larry Elliott & Richard J. Schroth

EMPLOYEE VIEW OF LONG-TERM INCENTIVES

Long-term incentives, especially in the form of stock options, are important to the executive ranks. This perspective has changed dramatically due to recent downturns in the market. Previously, executives expected to receive the ability to exercise options and immediately reap the financial reward of the spread between the option price and the actual stock price. Now, the same people are just as likely to ask for cash.

On a smaller scale, the availability of equity rewards has filtered through the hierarchy of the organization. All employees who receive long-term incentives view them as a means to accumulate wealth. This type of incentive became more popular among employees during the boom of the 1990s when the increased availability of information and the growth in the market fueled interest in the mechanisms of the market.

EMPLOYER VIEW OF LONG-TERM INCENTIVES

Currently, employers find long-term incentives, especially stock options, to be a complicated subject. Stock option abuse is under heavy scrutiny on several fronts. As a result of the disclosure of abuse, the two major accounting ruling bodies, the Financial Accounting Standards Board (FASB) and the International Accounting Standards (IAS), now have measures where stock options are recorded in a company's financial statements. They require that options be expensed at the time of issue according to the Black-Scholes (or other valuation techniques) model, which is used to derive a valuation for stock options traded on public markets. The Black-Scholes model takes into account a company's stock volatility and interest rates and determines what an option would be worth after a specified period of time.

BEST PRACTICE

Many companies, such as Coca Cola, began to expense stock options voluntarily well before the new change. However, many technology companies continue to oppose the immediate expensing of stock options. This opposition is primarily because the technology sector is the biggest issuer of stock options. The companies in this sector claim that following the FASB guidelines will obscure the actual operating results that are reported to the SEC. Legislators from Silicon Valley have sponsored bills to block the SEC from forcing companies to follow the FASB standard. Rest assured, this debate will continue for years to come.

Despite the current view of long-term incentives, they are still an important element of the total compensation package. They are instrumental in retaining existing talent and in attracting new talent at certain levels. Because of the elevated potential for change in regulations about stock options and other long-term incentives, compensation designers must remain current on appropriate usages. In this scenario, executive compensation specialists can be valuable partners in providing the implications and strategies in response to these changes.

BENEFITS

Benefits allow companies to help provide for the health and financial security of their employees. Benefits are usually explained at the time of hire and often require a waiting period before going into effect. Companies in the United States generally offer the same types of benefits, but as with other elements of compensation, benefit requirements differ throughout the world.

Benefits available at most companies include:

- **Health insurance**—covers illness and injuries. The rules differ between companies and can be quite complicated. Many companies also include dental insurance. Usually, the employee pays to enroll other family members.
- **Disability insurance**—covers employees in case an event leaves them unable to perform in the workplace.

- **Death benefits**—provide some financial security for the family of the employee in the event of an unfortunate demise.
- **Retirement benefits**—help provide for the employee when he or she reaches retirement age and actually retires. These benefits come in the form of either a pension or, more recently, a retirement account (401(k), profit-sharing, SERP, etc.). Retirement benefits are usually constrained by service time and legislative requirements.
- **Paid holidays and vacations**—allow time off for social and leisure activities. Holidays are normally available immediately. Vacations usually require minimum service time.
- **Educational assistance**—provides the employee an opportunity to grow both personally and professionally.
- **Sick/Personal Days**—allow employees time away when they are ill or need to assist an ill family member.

The benefit mix will vary for smaller organizations. Some companies allow the employee to choose between certain types of benefits and other forms of compensation.

EMPLOYEE VIEW OF BENEFITS

How the employee views benefits often depends on his or her specific needs. The view of benefits has also changed with the current work environment. Executives are less likely to be concerned about certain benefits than other employees.

Older workers are typically more concerned with benefits than younger employees. Veteran employees are approaching retirement, so the security of a retirement plan is attractive to them. Their bodies are also more likely to feel the effects of getting older which adds to the importance of health insurance.

Until they start having families, younger employees tend to be unconcerned with benefits other than vacations and educational assistance. Often, health care is not an issue, and retirement seems so far away. Once families begin to appear, benefits begin to increase in importance for these employees. They are specifically interested in death benefits and health insurance because they are committed to providing for their children's well being.

Often, executives do not view benefits in the same manner as other employees. The discrepancy in perception is due in part to the tax treatments and restrictions on the value of certain types of benefits. Also, benefits are a much less substantial piece of an executive compensation package.

EMPLOYER VIEW OF BENEFITS

Benefits are a cost of doing business. Employers know that their employees will be more productive if they feel secure and protected. However, the availability of benefits can be somewhat a point of contention between employers and employees. This situation occurs because the employees do not often understand the cost of providing the benefits they seek.

Despite the expense, companies can be rewarded for offering a substantial benefit package. Time away from work can also help employees be more productive when they are on the job. Health insurance can contribute directly to the level of productivity by decreasing the amount of time employees are ill or worried about ill children. Another benefit that can directly contribute to the success of the employer is educational assistance that improves the skill sets of employees.

Benefits are also a method for companies to be socially responsible. Because the United States views health care and retirement differently than the rest of the world, the social arrangement puts the onus on employers to subsidize health care and retirement.

As part of the total compensation package, benefits can serve multiple purposes. Benefits can serve to both attract and retain talent. Their purpose typically depends on the target employee group and the choice of benefits.

PERQUISITES

Everything else that contributes to the design of compensation package is called a perquisite. Perquisites are typically less tangible than other types of compensation. Often the value of a perquisite to the employee is not equivalent to the cost to the company. (Usually the employee places a much higher value on it).

Perquisites can range from golf club memberships to box seats to free soft drinks or subsidized parking. The most common perquisites are mobile phones and corporate cars. Obviously, the types of perquisites offered to executives and the rest of the employee population differ. Nonexecutives are offered small things that may make their lives more convenient.

EMPLOYEE VIEW OF PERQUISITES

Employees like perquisites. They contribute to the "psychic income" of employees. Because perquisites are often more personalized than other elements of compensation, they contribute to the employee's sense of well being. Typical employees do not necessarily view perquisites as an essential element of compensation, but rather as the cherry on top of the sundae.

Certain types of employees do view perquisites as an essential part of the compensation package. One of these groups is technology workers in general and those in relatively young companies in particular. This group of employees enjoys a slightly different work setting than the typical corporate work force. The most important perquisite for them is to be different—they want to be able to alter their workspace, to dress differently, to work abnormal hours. They also appreciate the availability of a recreational activity break in order to allow themselves to refocus on the task at hand.

Executives also have a different view of perquisites than the traditional employee. They view perquisites as a contributor to their status and as a supplement to benefits. Because of their perceived importance to the company, executives expect preferential treatment such as first-class airline seats and front row seats to cultural and sporting events. Executives also expect to receive supplemental benefits to offset benefit shortfalls caused by loss of retirement at a previous employer or tax disadvantages on other benefits. Often, executives receive financial planning services to assist them with more complicated estate situations.

EMPLOYER VIEW OF PERQUISITES

Employers like perquisites as well because the economic benefit typically exceeds the cost. Usually, large companies can purchase items and services used as perquisites at an extremely reduced rate. Certain industries, such as technology, have historically been fairly egalitarian in the availability of perquisites, but most companies tend to distribute availability along hierarchical lines.

Like stock options, perquisites are under scrutiny. Some companies, particularly startups in the technology sector, have been forced to limit perquisites due to funding issues. Other companies and their CEOs are under legal investigation due to excessive perquisites.

Although perquisites can be vague in nature, they are still an important element in the total compensation package. They contribute to all three goals of compensation – to attract, retain, and motivate talent. They do this by enhancing the corporate culture and by making the employee feel special. Care should be taken to create a well-defined perquisite program with proper "optics" to mitigate against any future problems.

All five elements (base salary, short-term incentives, long-term incentives, benefits, and perquisites) can work in concert to provide the organization with an abundant supply of motivated employees. How these elements are weighted can and should be fluid depending on organizational needs. Ideally, the weighting of the elements should fit the needs of the employee the organization is trying to attract, retain, or motivate.

QUESTIONS IN COMPENSATION DESIGN

Before beginning a foray into the design of a compensation package, the designers should ask themselves questions about the fit of the package into the needs of the organization. Some examples follow:

- How do we design the organization and manage the pay systems needed to attract, retain, and motivate the type of talent the company needs?
- Is the organization willing to customize the total package to meet the needs of the labor force?
- How should a diverse workgroup be managed?
- How is the compensation package going to align with organizational strategy?

HOW IS COMPENSATION TYPICALLY EXPRESSED?

Compensation usually is itemized by the element of the total package. The value of each element is expressed as a percentage of the base salary. An example using two executives with base salaries of $100,000 and $500,000 can be found in the following table.

Table 1-A

Executive's Base Salary	$100,000	$500,000
Base Salary	100%	100%
Short-term Incentives	30%	50%
Long-term incentives	50%	100%
Benefits	25%	10%
Perquisites	3%	5%
Total Package	208%	265%

Alternately, some companies express each element as a percentage of the total compensation. The previous example expressed in this manner is displayed in the following table.

Table 1-B

Total Package	$208,000	$1,325,000
Base Salary	48%	39%
Short-term Incentives	14%	19%
Long-term incentives	24%	39%
Benefits	12%	4%
Perquisites	2%	2%
Total Package	100%	100%

WHAT AFFECTS TOTAL COMPENSATION?

Many different factors contribute to the design of the compensation package. These factors include:

- **Job responsibilities**—consist of the type of work and the amount of responsibility the employee holds. Of substantial importance are management of other people and influence on the fulfillment of the corporate strategy.
- **Industry**—determines baselines for job responsibilities and wage rates.
- **Economics of the labor market**—determine the availability of talented replacements and the market rate for a given talent level. Both the availability and the rate are driven by the law of supply and demand.
- **Company size**—determines the complexity of job responsibilities (especially at the corporate officer level) and the amount of resources available to the company.

- **Company performance**—determines the needs of the organization as well as the resources available.
- **Executive performance**—provides a track record and baseline for performance. A strong track record removes the uncertainty associated with a particular individual.
- **Organizational culture**—determines what elements of the package are most appropriate.
- **Cost issues**—provide the financial constraints of the package. These issues may include time, implementation, funding, compliance, budgeting, cost control, and support staff.
- **Rules and regulations**—provide guidelines that a compensation package must meet.

These factors all contribute to the complexity of designing the compensation package. However, these factors are affected by other outside forces.

In addition, when designing a total rewards program, external and internal factors may need to be considered. Some of those factors to be considered are listed below.

- Internal
  - Corporate philosophy
  - Corporate mission
  - Business Strategy
  - Human resources philosophy
  - Costs/resource availability and strategy
  - Total rewards philosophy and strategy
  - Corporate culture
  - Shareholder expectations
  - Corporate structure
- External
  - Community culture
  - Competition
  - Economics
  - Industry characteristics
  - Labor market
  - Legal/regulatory
  - Technology
  - Globalization

CHALLENGES IN DESIGNING THE TOTAL COMPENSATION PACKAGE

Because companies must respond to today's needs, as well as hedge against future uncertainties, designing any business process is difficult. Compensation is no different. The process of predicting future needs while also coping with today's needs is what differentiates the successful companies from the unsuccessful.

Because the world is facing unprecedented risks, many companies are experiencing new challenges that distract from development for the future. The global environment is unlike any ever experienced by modern business. Although showing some recent stirrings of life, the market in the United States is in its fourth straight down year. The post-9/11 world seems more unstable with military involvement in Afghanistan and Iraq, terror threats, and dilemmas in business ethics, government, and sports. Japan has suffered through a long and persistent recession and Europe is facing financial crisis due to the increasing age of its citizens, huge pension obligations, and the inability of individual countries (in the Euro zone, *i.e.*, Germany) to devalue their currency in order to spur economic growth. The United States is also facing difficulties relating to an aging population facing the realities of delayed retirement.

Despite the uncertain global environment, companies need to anticipate which forces will shape the future of compensation. These forces, which are becoming apparent today, will be drivers for compensation design for the next two to five years and possibly beyond.

TALENT SHORTAGE

Despite the current concern about the unemployment rate, the actual employment level in the United States is remarkably high. According to Department of Labor statistics, the total employment in May of 2003 is within a few hundred thousand (out of 137+ million) of an all-time high. Not only are employment levels high, but technological advances have increased productivity to new heights.

Much of the growth in workforce requirements has come from the increasing requirement for knowledge workers. The requirement has grown as the integration of technology has permeated the business world. This segment of the labor market is important because of the technical skills that create a high demand for its members. The demand has forced companies to compete for talent in a seller's market or find alternative ways to fill needs.

As a result of the high demand and resultant high wage rates in the United States, many companies have opted to move knowledge jobs offshore. Between these actions and the market downturns, the market for knowledge workers has stabilized somewhat. Despite these labor market corrections, knowledge workers still command a premium. The challenge for the compensation professional is to design a package for workers who do not necessarily share the same requirements as traditional workers. This group on the whole strives for quality of life and puts an emphasis on time for community, security, and personal growth.

DIVERSE WORKFORCE

The workforce in the United States has never been more diverse. The workforce is now comprised of men and women of every race, age, orientation, and background. Designing a "one-size-fits-all" compensation package would be useless.

Age is now the primary differentiation point when designing compensation. Americans are living and working longer. The difference in perspectives on life, motivation, and talents based on age differences causes friction in the workplace and the need for divergent compensation strategies.

The oldest group of employees is comprised of people born prior to the 1940s. They have a sense of duty grounded in World War II. This group has had long careers and expects to reap the fruits of their previous labor. Because of the increases in the cost of living and sheer boredom, many members of this group who were previously retired have reentered the work force.

Baby Boomers are the next group. They have developed a taste for material wealth, but are now trying to redefine their lives as they approach retirement age. Because of market downturns, many in this group do not expect to fully retire. Baby Boomers are in an awkward stage of their life cycle because the leading edge of the group is feeling the effects of age, while the professionals at the tail end are still chasing their young children.

Gen Xers are the first group to grow up in a knowledge-based world. As such, they view work and life differently than the generations that came before. According to the previous generations, work ethics have changed; but, in fact, the change is primarily in the approach toward completing the task at hand. Gen Xers believe in a life outside of work and have different motivations.

One thing to note about money is that it's usually easy to buy survival, but it is much harder to buy social ties and entertainment. Especially Entertainment with a capital E—the kind that gives life meaning…Money remains a powerful thing, but is still just a proxy for other more fundamental motivating factors.
—Linus Torvolds

Millennials (Gen Y) are just entering the workforce. They have never lived in a world without mass-marketed computers. This group is highly skilled and very social. They also have a global view that is unsurpassed by the previous generations. As they are still in a very idealistic stage of their life cycles, community and social responsibility are very important to them.

In a very broad sense, the approaches toward employment can be divided into the older groups (Baby Boomers and older) and the younger groups (Gen X and the Millennials). Until recently, the older group primarily experienced careers inside one company. The younger group expects to have nearly 10 different employers during the course of an average career.

The challenge for compensation specialists now: to understand the needs of four generations instead of just two. Other compensation challenges are a result of increased workplace diversity. The level of complexity in compensation packages will only increase as they expand to meet a wider variety of needs.

NATURE OF WORK

Businesses are adapting to the increasing use of technology. This adaptation is causing more and more work to become knowledge based. The very nature of knowledge-based work allows and encourages fluidity in organizations. As a result, most corporate work has become project-centric. The preeminent method of gaining results has become the project-based team. These teams are often assembled to focus solely on the project at hand. As such, they often contain members of different functional arenas. These project teams have become an outstanding method for the cross-pollination of formerly siloed knowledge (where one individual was charged with becoming specialized in one facet of technology or business).

Other forces are changing the nature of work. One is the enlargement of the service economy. As more jobs in the United States are created in this sector, an even greater premium will be placed on customer service. Another important trend affecting the nature of work is outsourcing. Outsourcing is dependent on the ability to transfer pieces of information to specialists who can fulfill the corporate needs in a more cost-efficient manner.

GLOBALIZATION

With the advances in communication, the world has become a smaller place. Businesses now compete all over the world. Corporations are entering new markets everywhere and must face the challenges of those markets. Compensation plans must now be constructed to meet the regulations of multiple countries. These regulations may be tax laws or pension requirements. Care must be taken because regulations in countries such as Brazil and Germany impede the termination of employees, even with just cause.

Mobility is another contributor to the effects of globalization. People and work have both become more mobile. In the current environment, companies can hire locally, import talent, or move the job to a location where talent is available. This capability has made compensation even more strategically important because the advice of a compensation expert can lead to a major financial impact.

COMMUNICATIONS TECHNOLOGY

Advances in communications technology have aided globalization as well as affected the labor market. The adoption of the Internet has outpaced the adoption cycles of all previous technological forms of communication. For development of compensation packages, this is both good and bad. Because of the capabilities of modern communication, employees are more informed about compensation choices, and companies find the release of information easier. Unfortunately, not all companies use new technology efficiently, which leads to employee frustration with the level of information they are receiving. Another difficulty with the availability of information is the high volume of misinformation. This misinformation creates a misalignment of expectations that leads to compensation dissatisfaction or to job change.

These forces, as well as other emergent issues, will shape the development of compensation packages for the near to midrange future. Regardless of the externalities, solid compensation structures will be required to attract, retain, and motivate talented employees.

Trends in compensation package design

During this time of uncertainty, many employers are trying new ideas in compensation to improve their competitive position in the labor marketplace. The trial-and-error period is spawning several trends in compensation, which follow:

- **Less reliance on traditional sources of market data.** Companies are beginning to gather their own data from many different sources to better build their own picture of the labor market.
- **Different pay strategies for different types of work.** Employers have begun targeting compensation packages for differing classes of employees.
- **Well-defined strategies and systems for managing the pay of nonpermanent workers.** As companies become more aggressive in the use of contract and contingent workers – a result of trying to mitigate the current mass hire/layoff cycle – they will become better at handling the compensation of those workers. This is also an area where new legislation may arise as a result of the increase in this type of labor.
- **More global positioning.** Jobs will become more global in nature as companies look throughout the world for low-cost, high-value labor to perform in the highly transportable information economy.
- **New approaches to valuing jobs in the workplace.** Jobs are increasingly becoming value-proposition based, which is further detailed as follows:

Employment and compensation are increasingly a result of a value proposition between the employer and the employee. Employers are making a greater effort to satisfy the needs of its employees to provide a reasonable level of job security and to better communicate expectations of both the employer and the employee. In return, employees understand that the times of the free ride at work are gone. Employers expect a measurable return on the investment that they have made in the employees themselves. In his book analysis of return on human resources, Jac Fitz-Enz has come to the conclusion that employers will use an increasing amount of metrics to better evaluate the return on investment in human capital. Through orientation and other informative initiatives, employers will provide a thorough explanation of these metrics to the employees.

THE FUTURE OF TOTAL COMPENSATION STRATEGIES

Total compensation strategies will be used to attract, retain, and motivate talented employees who promote the desired corporate culture. As organizations become more sophisticated, they begin to understand that the corporate culture and organizational strategies must be aligned. The ability to effectively design multiple compensation strategies is a key piece of the harmonization of strategy and culture.

Well-designed compensation strategies are also required to cope with the riskier economic environment. Fluidity in the labor market is a primary cause of organizational risk. Successful companies, such as Southwest Airlines, take calculated risks in the area of compensation to build a competitive advantage in human resources.

CHAPTER TWO

WHAT'S NEW IN COMPENSATION

OBJECTIVE

This chapter seeks to identify how current changes in the global, political, economic, social, and demographic environments will affect compensation. Utilizing a top-down approach, the chapter will first discuss corporate governance, boardroom trends, and the compensation of directors. Logically, the compensation of executives and the all-employee workforce will follow. The chapter will conclude with big picture trends and a spotlight on "customized compensation."

KEY POINTS

◊ The new emphasis on corporate governance has prompted a change from previous compensation techniques to one that involves more stringent levels of accountability.

◊ Compensation packages must be sculpted to lead to increased motivation, retention, and attraction of top-level talent.

◊ The customized compensation approach attempts to better align individual employees' compensation with their needs.

Over the last several years, the business world has suffered from increased amounts of stress on the workforce. Factors such as international politics, corporate scandals, and a weak economy have affected enormous change in corporate governance, culture, and business process. These changes will directly affect how employees are compensated in the future.

THE BOARD

The board of directors holds a special place of responsibility in a corporation. The board serves as the interface between the owners (stockholders) and upper management. Even so, the function of the board has not always been well understood by the general public. At times, the intermingling of members from various companies has even led some to perceive the board as simply an "old boys" network with its economic advantages. This view began to dissipate in the 1990s, however, as more and more of middle class America became involved in the financial markets. People became more aware of individual members as increases in both the speed and access to information shed light on specific companies and board members. Today more than ever before, in the wake of a market downturn and numerous corporate scandals, boards are being examined more closely.

Historically, board of director compensation has been based on factors such as the expertise and background of the individual. Compensation for board members typically includes a mix of cash and equity. For example, in 2000, average equity compensation for board members of the largest corporations in the United States was approximately 60 percent of the total compensation package. For board members in the technology sector, the equity portion of compensation was even higher. Further, there has been a move away from stock options to restricted stock. This move has not only been a result of better dynamics of restricted stock, but also the perception–*they don't tempt directors the way options do*–to inflate earnings.

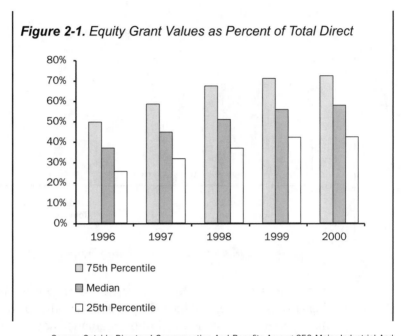

Figure 2-1. *Equity Grant Values as Percent of Total Direct*

☐ 75th Percentile
▨ Median
☐ 25th Percentile

Source: Outside Directors' Compensation And Benefits Among 350 Major Industrial And Service Companies: 2001 Update, Mercer, June 2001.

A rash of corporate scandals have changed the way many view corporate governance. As a result of Sarbanes-Oxley, legislation intended to push corporate governance reform, new measures to assure the independence and the validity of the audit have been put into place. Companies are now expected to have fully independent accounting and compensation committees. Although board members may serve on a variety of committees, usually compensation is the same within a corporation regardless of actual responsibilities. This holds true for the crucial audit and compensation committees where, under new legislation, members of the audit committee can be held liable.

In addition to significant changes in the form and amounts of equity compensation, board members are now receiving more cash incentives and retainer fees. Similar changes are expected to continue as further progression of corporate governance influences board of director compensation.

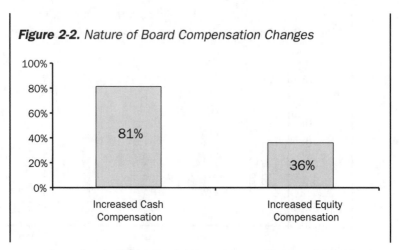

Figure 2-2. Nature of Board Compensation Changes

Source: Emerging Trends in Board of Director Compensation, Mercer, Feb. 2003.

Corporations have come to accept the need for outside board members to ensure independence. Corporations are also looking for specific experience and skills. In addition, regulation now mandates required skills and backgrounds for at least some of the audit committee members. Companies now expect their board members to take a more active role in providing guidance for the CEO and the rest of the company, a requirement that has narrowed the available talent pool.

In addition to these company factors, fewer potential board members are willing to accept positions. While some cannot meet the increased requirements placed on them by the company, others are simply seeking to reduce their exposure to risk. In addition, board members that are both willing and capable are limiting themselves to fewer boards to better fulfill their respective responsibilities.

Table 2-A. *Factors Increasing Board Compensation*

Decreased Supply	Increased Demand
Fewer qualified	New committees formed
Fewer independent	Fewer willing to take seats due to additional risk and liability
Fewer eligible to serve on multiple boards	More stringent requirements on qualifications
Incorporation of diversity	Shareholder pressure to change
	Increase in time served

As the supply and demand curves for board talent shift in opposite directions, board compensation can be expected to increase. Retainers will continue to rise as companies attempt to attract and keep key individuals. Less focus on meeting fees and a greater emphasis on the evaluation of board performance, particularly at the individual level, can also be expected. Retirement plans for board members will dwindle and may eventually disappear as retirement becomes less relevant for these individuals.

The composition of the boardroom is also changing. Boards will get larger in order to absorb more outside leadership–and the increase in individual requirements, responsibility, and scrutiny will greatly reduce the number of active CEOs serving. The boardroom, on average, will continue to get younger and more diverse.

EXECUTIVES

As the business environment has changed, the approach and attitudes toward employment have changed as well. Historically, companies placed a great deal of emphasis on loyalty. Top executives who remained loyal to the company could expect to be rewarded over the long run. Today, as the bargaining power of executives has substantially increased, loyalty has been somewhat extracted from the equation.

The relationship between the company and the executive is becoming much more symbiotic. Thus, compensation packages must be designed so that the executive, acting in his or her own best interest, best benefits the company. While politically it may seem somewhat counterintuitive to align the executive in this manner, it is precisely this methodology that may prevent misconduct in the future. This concept, when used with proper pay-for-performance incentives, can lead to increased motivation, retention, and attraction of top-level talent.

Many times the pay difference between top management and the workforce is a source of contention among employees. This pressure is further increased during bear markets where executive compensation may appear more excessive due to superior performance. Executive retirement plans, highly publicized in recent years, also attract increased attention in a down market. Widely reported scandals at companies such as Tyco, Enron, and WorldCom had negative effects on public and shareholder sentiment. In the wake of the dot.com downslide, corporate scandal and an overly uncertain political environment, public outcry over abuses—and perceived abuses—in executive pay has prompted new legislation and corrective measures.

These changes sparked a debate over the use of stock options and other forms of equity compensation. Although decreasing as a percentage of total compensation packages, long-term incentives still account for the majority of an executive's total compensation.

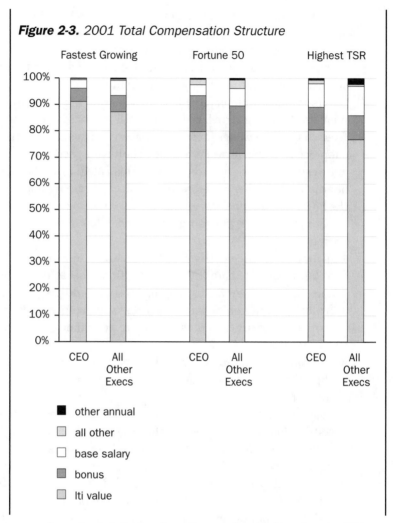

Figure 2-3. *2001 Total Compensation Structure*

Source: *America's Top Guns Survey,* Resources Consulting Group, December 2001.

Today's mandatory stock option expensing and increased concern over dilution has decreased both the use and depth of stock option programs. According to the Mercer 2002 CEO Compensation Survey, the number of CEOs receiving stock options fell by over 6 percent from 2001 to 2002. While fewer CEOs receiving stock options indicate a move away from stock options, the decline in value of both grants and exercised option gains also can be attributed to recent market performance. Currently, 50 percent of executives are dealing with some form of underwater options. An underwater option is an outstanding option where the option price (or strike price) is above the stock's current price. These early trends can be expected to continue as more companies move away from stock options toward restricted stock and other forms of long-term incentives.

Since stock options have lost their favorable accounting treatment, the best long-term incentive vehicles are those with a budgeted fixed charge to earnings for awards that are "full value" versus solely "appreciative" in nature. Performance unit plans, performance share, and restricted stock awards fall into this category. Although each alternative has advantages, restricted stock is gaining popularity as the best alternative.

Companies are choosing restricted stock for the following reasons:

- Although restricted stock awards require immediate dilution of Earnings Per Share (EPS), the dilution is set at the grant date and does not vary as restrictions lapse. In addition, companies typically grant significantly fewer RSAs than other types of long-term incentives (*i.e.* options), therefore positioning executives for less dilution.
- The long-term nature of these restricted stock awards serves to align the goals of the executive with the long-term vision of the company.
- Restricted stock awards have an automatic value at grant with restrictions on the sale or transfer of the stock for a fixed period of time. Therefore, the executive immediately owns the stock, has voting rights with the stock, and is eligible to receive dividends.
- Restricted stock awards have a high retention value due to forfeiture of the stock following an early departure.

Although opponents of restricted stock argue that the lapse of restrictions as time passes does not motivate the executive to surpass performance goals, customized techniques for restricted stock awards allow enough flexibility to remedy this situation. Alternatives include accelerated vesting to award key employees for exceptional performance, as well as an election—IRC Section 83(b)—which allows the recipient to choose to be taxed at the value of the shares at award rather than when the restrictions lift.

Although typically only an executive's long-term incentive package is affected by the ebb and flow of the market, the fixed portion of executive total direct compensation has been affected as well. The most immediate impact is the more restrained upward movement in recent CEO salary levels. Base pay increased by only two percent and more companies decided against salary raises in 2002. Even so, the improvement in performance by businesses did translate directly to increased remuneration for executives as bonuses for CEO's increased by approximately the same ratio as companies' net incomes.

A *Corporate Board Member* magazine survey of 882 CEOs and directors reported the following results:

- 62% are against any move that would require executives to hold all or most of their stock options for the entire time they are employed
- 64% favor the certification of financial results
- 77% favor tougher penalties for errant executives
- 48% endorse shareholder approval of stock option plans
- 20% of CEOs stated they would likely resign if all the recently proposed governance reforms are OK

Companies faced similar volatile markets and depressed stock option values in the 1970s. Macroeconomic factors effectively left options worthless at a time when companies were overly concerned with attraction and retention. Many times companies simply added pay packages on top of existing plans. Stock option programs were not broad based and overhang was not an issue. Overhang is a measure of potential dilution from stock compensation plans. It is defined as the number of shares in outstanding grants plus those remaining available for future grants divided by common shares outstanding.

During the 1980s, increases in foreign competition caused the strength of labor unions to decline as benefits continued to increase as a percentage of total compensation. Health care and retirement accounted for much of this increase. To control these costs, employees were asked to make larger contributions to benefits such as health insurance, and defined benefit plans declined in favor of defined contribution plans.

The 1990s were a period of massive economic growth and low unemployment. Inflation stayed surprisingly low and wage rates did not increase much. Benefits costs represented an increasingly larger percentage of compensation cost as wages and other forms of direct compensation retained a larger portion. Compensation, especially toward the end of the decade, began to include more pay-for-performance and flexibility features.

Today, executives are more highly compensated and dilution is a huge concern. Many believe options are a get-rich-quick management scheme. Executives themselves argue that fluctuations in short-to-intermediate-term option values are not related to performance. Thus, companies are looking to regain shareholder trust amidst confusion and ongoing corporate corruption. The challenge is not in the decision between which long-term incentive vehicle is the best, but rather in the metrics that link the executive to shareholder wealth creation. Companies that manage to incorporate measures that better link executives will benefit from higher productivity and shareholder approval.

Figure 2-4. *Overhang & Dilution Level Concern*

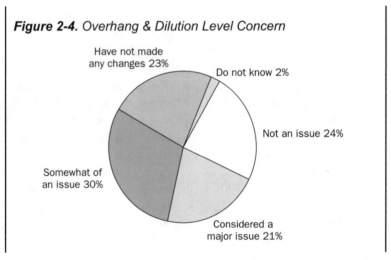

Source: Future of Equity – 2003 Update, Mercer, June 2003

Attractive alternatives do exist for stock options. These alternatives include the following broad classifications as described in *Stock Option Alternatives: A Strategic and Technical Guide to Long-Term Incentives,* published by WorldatWork:

- Full Value Awards
  - Restricted Stock Awards
  - Founders Stock
  - Discounted Stock Options

- Appreciation Awards
  - Stock Appreciation Rights (SARs)
  - Phantom Stock
  - Formula Value Shares
- Goal-Based Shares
  - Performance Shares
- Goal-Based Cash
  - Performance Unit Plans
- Other Programs

Restricted stock awards

Restricted stock awards are a grant of stock by an employer to an employee in which the employee's rights to the stock are subject to some type of restriction and risk of forfeiture. Restrictions most often include an employment or length-of-service restriction, also known as time-lapse restricted stock (*i.e.*, vesting over a three to five year period). Typically, the employee may not pledge, sell, or transfer the shares of stock until the restrictions lapse; however, the employee receives dividends and voting rights during the restriction period. Once the stated restrictions lapse, the employee obtains full ownership of the unrestricted shares that may be pledged, sold, or transferred. In the event the employee does not meet the stated restrictions, however, the shares are forfeited. (Figures 2-5 and 2-6)

Figure 2-5. Restricted Stock works as follows ...

Timing	Years	
	1	5
Restricted Stock	Grant	Restrictions Lapse
Fair Market Value:	$5	$10
Dividends:	$0	$1.00
Executive Investment:	$0	$0
Executive Gain:	$0	$11.00 (Ordinary Income)
Executive Tax [1]:	$0	$3.65 Tax Due
	($10 X 35%) + ($1.00 X 15%)	
Executive Net Gain: (After Tax)	$0	$7.35 Net Gain

(1) Assumes the executive is subject to an ordinary income tax rate of 35%. If an 83(b) election was made within 30 days of the award, the executive would be taxed on the fair value of the stock at grant as ordinary income, with subsequent appreciation treated as a capital gain. Dividend is taxed at long-term capital gains rate. 83(b) elections are not typically with a high prices stock because the executive cannot recover taxes paid at grant if he or she forfeits the shares or if the shares decrease in value.

Figure 2-6. Restricted Stock

Key Provisions
- Outright grant of shares to executives with restrictions as to sale, transfer and pledging
- Restrictions lapse over a period of time (e.g., three to five years)
- As restrictions lapse, executive has unrestricted shares which he or she may sell, transfer or pledge
- If executive terminates employment, all unvested shares are forfeited
- During restriction period, executive receives dividends and can vote the shares

Earnings Impact
- Fair market value at grant charged to earnings over restriction period
- Subsequent appreciation not charged to earnings
- Immediate dilution of EPS for total shares granted

Tax Impact on Executive[1]
- At grant—no tax
- As restrictions lapse--the current market value of vested shares taxed as ordinary income
- Dividends received during restriction period taxed as long-term cap. Gains (15%)

Tax Impact on Company[1]
- At grant—no tax deduction
- As restrictions lapse— company receives tax deduction equal to executive's ordinary income
- At sale—no tax deduction
- Dividends paid during restriction period are not deductible

Advantages
- No executive investment required
- Promotes immediate stock ownership
- Charge to earnings is fixed at time of grant
- If stock appreciates, company's tax deduction exceeds fixed charge to earnings
- Aligns executive's interests with shareholders
- Recognizable to most executives
- Offers executive potentially long-term appreciation as company grows

Disadvantages
- Immediate dilution of EPS
- Executive may incur tax liability before shares are sold
- Executive may pay tax (at vesting) at a higher stock price than the date of sale

(1) Assumes 83(b) election is not made. If an 83(b) is made, executive recognizes income on the date the restricted stock was issued, and the company receives an immediate tax deduction for the initial value of the shares (but not for subsequent appreciation during the restriction period); dividends paid during the restriction period are not deductible.

BEST PRACTICE

In the summer of 2004, Microsoft opted to change its long-term incentive program. All employees are now granted restricted stock units, which would vest over a five-year period. Executives are eligible to receive "share-performance stock awards" based on three-year nonoverlapping performance periods. The program was intended to aid in the retention of employees and provide a recognizable long-term compensation value. With the passage of the American Jobs Creation Act (AJCA), this plan required tweaking, but Microsoft (a company always ahead of the HR curve) has met the challenge head-on and continues to attract, retain, and motivate great talent.

Founders stock

Founders stock is stock granted very early in a company's business cycle, whereby key employees (founders) purchase shares of common stock at a nominal value. Similar to restricted stock awards, there are usually restrictions attached—typically continued employment. In the event the employee (founder) does not meet the stated restrictions, the shares are forfeited. The idea behind founders stock is to provide an ownership opportunity for executives while the stock is at a deep discount.

Discounted stock options

A discounted stock option, or DSO, is a standard nonqualified stock option with a grant or exercise price lower than the fair market value on the date of grant. The "discounting" provides what is, in effect, immediate ownership—similar to a restricted stock award. As a result, it protects its grantees from market volatility in an effort to enhance retention. As with other long-term plans, vesting requirements are typically attached. Unfortunately, provisions in the recently enacted American Jobs Creation Act make the use of DSOs very unfavorable.

Stock appreciation rights

A stock appreciation right, or more commonly referred to as a "SAR," is a long-term incentive vehicle in which the corporation grants an executive the right to receive a dollar amount of value equal to the future appreciation of its shares. A SAR is typically exercised by the grantee after a specific vesting period. U.S. companies (operating in foreign countries where the tax and/or other local laws precluded the use of stock options) have used SARs extensively. Again, the AJCA has created an interesting problem with SARs; at vesting, there is a tax to the executive. As a result, most new SAR plans will have cliff vesting versus the more traditional graded.

Phantom stock

Phantom stock is a long-term incentive arrangement in which the executive receives the appreciation in the book, fair-market, or formula value over a set period of time. Phantom shareholders do not own actual stock and typically do not have voting rights; however, they are usually eligible to receive dividends or their equivalent. Phantom stock is generally utilized by privately-held companies that want to be competitive but cannot or do not want to grant actual stock to executives. As with SARs, the AJCA is having practitioners go to cliff vesting to match the taxable event with executive liquidity.

Formula value shares

A Formula Value Plan is a plan in which compensation is earned when the formula value of the shares increases above the formula value at the time the units were initially granted. The grantee's primary incentive is to increase company/business unit performance and thus increase the formula value of the shares owned. This type of plan is often designed as a "book value" appreciation plan.

Performance share plan

A Performance Share Plan is a stock (or stock unit) grant award plan contingently granted upon the achievement of certain predetermined external or internal performance goals. These goals must be met during a specified period (*e.g.,* three to five years) before the recipient has rights to the stock. Further, the share value is linked to either the fair market value of the employer's stock or a specific book/formula value. Thus, there is a double incentive for the grantee: (1) to achieve the goals established and (2) to work toward a higher stock price.

Performance unit plan

A Performance Unit Plan (PUP) is a unit award plan contingently granted on the achievement of certain predetermined external or internal performance goals over a specified period (typically three to five years) before the recipient has a right to the unit. Unlike a Performance Share Plan (PSP), the unit value rarely has any tieback to stock price and the actual award payment is typically paid in cash.

In addition to the programs already described, there are several other long-term incentive and/or deferral programs that have become popular now that stock option expensing is mandatory. Specifically, programs such as performance–based stock options, index options, economic value plans, and various forms of nonqualified deferred compensation have become more palatable to corporations looking for the proper mix.

WORKFORCE

Over the last century, the workforce composition has changed from primarily a manufacturing force paid based on output to a service force paid for time. Compensation packages have matured from wage-only remuneration toward complex blends of wages, bonuses, benefits, and often equity. A variety of factors including the economy, labor movements, globalization, and political and social changes helped effect these changes.

Table 2-B. Developments in Compensation Packages–Wages, Time-off and Reimbursement; Health Care and Life Insurance Benefits; and Retirement and Savings Plans

	1900	1925	1950	1975	2000
Wages, time-off and reimbursement accounts	Wages	Wages; Paid holidays	Wages; Paid holidays and vacation	Wages and annual bonuses; Paid holidays, vacations, and personal leave	Wages, and supplements that tie pay to performance; Consolidated leave plan giving employee choice of days off; Unpaid family leave; Reimbursement account for child care expenses
Health care and life insurance benefits		Company doctor; Benevolent association death and disability benefits	Basic medical plan through Blue Cross-Blue Shield; Fixed amount life insurance and weekly disability benefit	Basic medical plan plus major medical through commercial insurer; Dental plan; Medicare; Life insurance varying with earnings; paid sick leave	Choice of medical plans including Health Maintenance Organizations (HMOs); Choice of dental, vision, and prescription drug plans; Medicare and retiree health insurance; Choice of life insurance amounts; paid sick leave
Retirement and savings plans			Social Security benefits available at age 65	Social Security benefits available at age 65, with reduced benefits at age 62; Defined benefit pension	Social Security full benefits available at age 67, with reduced benefits at age 62, for workers born in 1960 or later; Combination of pensions and 401(K) savings plans

Source: Compensation and Working Conditions, Fall 2001.

The approach toward workforce compensation has changed through several business cycles as performance metrics have fluctuated. Currently, work is primarily team-based and cooperative within service-based industries. As true within the executive ranks, employee loyalty has suffered in recent years. Much of the most recent disloyalty can be attributed to the economic downturn that left many companies dealing with overstaffing issues.

Increased competitive pressures have forced many companies to shift toward the use of contingent workers. As a result, human resources systems have had to redefine the employer-employee relationship to incorporate increased amounts of flexibility. This added flexibility has resulted in both benefits and costs.

Increased flexibility associated with increasing numbers of contingent workers has given managers additional strategy control mechanisms. The ability to control labor costs on variable rather than fixed basis is a tremendous benefit. Other perceived benefits of a contingent workforce include:

- Increased security/job opportunity for remaining workforce
- Increased work/life balance
- Easier for jobless workers to find a job

Even so, this process has forced many employees to identify themselves with their occupation rather than with the company they work for. This disconnect is also apparent in contingent worker compensation. Many workers must accept lower wages, decreased job advancement opportunities and a lack of fringe benefits in exchange for increased freedom. In addition, strong barriers may form between the contingent and core workforce. Additional costs include:

- Economic insecurity from lack of benefits
- Level and rate at which unemployment rises in a recession could increase
- Tendency to under invest in human capital
- Harder to meet affirmative action goals

Currently, compensation for full-time employees typically consists of a full range of elements including base salary, incentive pay, benefit, and even equity plans. Often the total package is based on some kind of performance pay. These plans have become increasingly more effective with the increased sophistication of performance measures. The usage of performance, as opposed to tenure, adds to the flexibility of the employer-employee relationship, which is further evidenced by nontraditional approaches to work arrangements.

Successful workforce compensation packages will incorporate flexibility and stress communication. By using novel approaches to benefits and perquisites, companies can find inexpensive ways to reward employees for performance. This allows for reduced dependence on cash and/or stock option usage without sacrificing attraction or retention. Some of the ways companies are meeting these challenges are:

- Compressed work weeks
- More casual workplace attire
- Telecommuting
- Child care
- Cafeteria benefit packages
- Flexible holidays

THE "BIG PICTURE"— TRENDS FOR THE FUTURE

Compensation is changing in response to developments at the macro level. These trends are broadly affecting compensation and can be divided into the following categories:

- Global business environment
- Changing work environment
- Moving pay gaps
- Technical innovations
- Changing legislation
- Demographic shifts

Over the years, businesses have learned to adequately respond to normal business cycles and inevitable economic retractions. Even so, the apex of the Internet bubble aftermath, Sept. 11th, corporate corruption, and ongoing war fears have forced the global economy to respond differently. These events have sparked an overwhelming desire for increased job security.

Companies are now looking to sustain talent by becoming more flexible by reacting quicker to employee needs. Organizations are increasingly more willing to allow employees to change locations, work part-time, or even alter their role in the company. In addition, companies are offering case-by-case incentives to key individuals while attempting to define themselves as a choice employer. These programs are focusing on quality-of-life issues that add value at a reasonable cost.

The work environment is also changing. Companies have invested heavily in human capital, and a greater emphasis on intellectual and knowledge-based skills has increased the cost of employee turnover. Today's employee is expected to be flexible and capable of performing job functions at a high level of competency. Organizations that terminate the wrong people may suffer from a lack of critical skills and a remaining disheartened workforce. To combat this problem, companies are using job/skill sharing, projects with reduced time commitment, and contractual arrangements to help manage costs.

In addition to the focus on retention, companies are more global and must manage international workforce compensation issues. Inefficiencies and additional costs add to problems created by new legislation and varying market conditions. Companies competing in this environment must establish equitable pay practices and effectively communicate career path opportunities.

In many ways, human resource system costs are directly related to the speed at which the organization can react to changing market conditions. Emerging technology will allow leading companies to react faster with better decisions. According to a 2002 Hewitt study, 72 percent of CEOs surveyed identified speed and agility as a critical aspect of their business plan to address intense market pressures. For this reason, the use of automated HR activities and the application of additional technology will continue to rise. These systems will reduce costs and allow management to make quicker, more informed HR decisions.

Trends are also emerging in workforce demographics. Baby Boomers, in addition to increased life expectancy and poor retirement savings levels, are causing the working population to get older. In 2006, half of the work force will be older than 50, and by 2017 more people will be exiting the workforce than entering. Even so, because we have shifted from a production economy into a service-based information economy, age and manual labor concerns are less of an issue. The challenge for companies will be to adequately retain experienced workers while balancing the needs of various age groups. As a result, workplace diversity and increased flexibility in compensation design can be expected to grow considerably.

Along with additional customizable features, compensation packages will continue to emphasize pay-for-performance incentives. Designed properly, these programs can be effectively utilized to:

- Increase performance
- Remain competitive
- Improve customer satisfaction
- Control labor costs

According to the 2002 WorldatWork annual *Total Salary Increase Budget Survey*, 65 percent of companies are offering employees some form of variable pay. Although stock awards are still very common, the use of variable pay, including individual awards, special recognition programs, group/team awards, and organization-wide awards is on the rise.

In addition to variable pay, companies are using sign-on, retention, spot, and employee referral bonuses to attract and retain talent. Companies choosing to communicate the dollar value of their employees' respective total compensation/benefit packages further underscore these efforts. Over time, more companies will engage in these types of marketing and communication efforts to help employees gain understanding and appreciation of organizational compensation philosophy and value.

SPOTLIGHT ON "CUSTOMIZED COMPENSATION"

Customized compensation is the application of masscustomization to compensation design.
—Future Perfect by Stanley Davis

The aging and increased diversity of today's workforce coupled with higher demand for work-life balance has created the need for increased flexibility. Corporate culture and demographics are also changing. In addition, companies must meet the needs of both domestic and international employees as more companies seek worldwide operation. Essentially, the one-size-fits-all approach to compensation lacks the ability to efficiently motivate a work force that is increasingly more dynamic.

Customized compensation works by finding the rewards that best motivate an individual employee and making them attainable. While cash may motivate some, others may prefer more time off. The customized compensation approach attempts to maximize motivation with reward systems that better align individual employees with their needs.

Although it may seem like the concept of different rewards for different employees is not internally equitable, the approach seeks to maximize motivation for each individual, which can be seen as internal equity as each employee is provided with equal opportunity.

Although certain benefit plans (*e.g.,* cafeteria plans) have addressed employee needs at the individual level, the customization approach has not yet been fully applied to compensation. Drawbacks include increased complexity in reporting, managing, and pay system design. In addition, companies may find it difficult to quantify various tradeoffs, and the relative emphasis of financial and nonfinancial rewards may vary between companies and employees.

Since the turn of the century, we have seen more developments in compensation than ever before. Compensation packages are getting more efficient and effective in maintaining the "golden rule" of compensation – attraction, retention, and motivation. The key is to continually evaluate and revise the package when appropriate.

CHAPTER THREE

DOES YOUR CURRENT COMPENSATION STRATEGY WORK?

OBJECTIVE

A compensation strategy may be letter perfect, but if it is not serving the goals of the organization, it is not working. This chapter discusses how to measure the effectiveness of your compensation system.

KEY POINTS

◊ Before implementing new ideas in compensation strategy, an evaluation of the current system should be made.
◊ Cost can significantly influence the design of a rewards program.
◊ The intent of a rewards package is to promote employee behavior that will become aligned with organizational goals.
◊ Each package should be individualized to maximize its effectiveness.

Total rewards concepts have been introduced. New developments in the total rewards have been discussed. **Now what?** None of this information matters if it is not implemented.

How do human resource professionals know when to use this knowledge? They know by observation of the employees, the management, the economy, the competition, and the world in general. They ask questions of management, peers, and employees. For example, HR might survey managers if more structure or more flexibility is needed for the compensation program and survey employees to determine if they feel they are motivated to perform better as a result of the way the compensation program is designed.

In times of change, the rewards system should be evaluated. If disjoints occur throughout the company, re-examine the system. Typical signs include:

- Mergers
- Employee apathy
- Changing labor market conditions
- New competitors in the market
- New management
- Redefinition of corporate goals
- New government regulations

Since changes occur continuously, human resource professionals must **always** be examining the total rewards system. Opportunities can be maximized when someone pays attention at a critical time and can capitalize on the chance.

BEST PRACTICE

Introducing merger mania in compensation

Company name:	AstroClutch
Problem faced by company:	The total rewards design process at Astro began as a result of the merger between Astro and Clutch in 1999. During the course of the merger, a human resources conference was held to discuss the new company's direction. To meet the challenges of combining the two cultures and two compensation systems of the formerly separate companies, a choice was made to go beyond the former compensation systems of either company.
Compensation solutions:	The human resources team decided to develop a new total rewards compensation program. They chose to develop a flexible system that allowed the company to become "an employer of choice." Designing a "new" program fostered positive feelings about the merger allowing Astro and Clutch to be a part of something new rather than trying to adopt one of their current plans.
Benefit to company:	The new system enabled the company to alter the employer/employee relationship into a partnership. Employees were excited and motivated not only throughout the merger process, but about the future direction of the company.

Before implementing new ideas in compensation strategy, a baseline evaluation of the current system should be conducted. As explained in Chapter One, the compensation package is a piece of the entire design of the organization. Therefore, the examination of the compensation strategy should begin with an examination of the organization. This review must examine the needs of the entire organization and how the compensation strategy is aligned with those needs. A thorough evaluation will highlight the elements that are working and those that are not.

Before discussing the evaluation of a total rewards program, a review of the total rewards process is in order. This process can be used as reference throughout the total rewards evaluation and as a framework for any change implementations. Any review of the total rewards design process must first examine the factors affecting it.

FACTORS INFLUENCING THE TOTAL REWARDS DESIGN PROCESS

Internal and external factors influence the rewards program design process. Some of the external factors, including globalization, technology, and labor market characteristics, were discussed in Chapter One. Internal factors such as corporate culture, cost issues, and ownership expectations are detailed below.

ORGANIZATIONAL CULTURE

DEFINITION

The culture of the organization is defined as the shared beliefs and values of the members of an organization.

The culture is built around a set of shared assumptions. Members of the organization share values and behaviors. Often, the organization may have cultural symbols to further bind the members together. Various ceremonies and rites such as award ceremonies or public recognition may also serve to reinforce the culture.

Cultures come in different varieties. Some companies may be more entrepreneurial, while others may be more bureaucratic. The culture of successful companies typically binds employees together with the same goals. Southwest Airlines is famous for its "us against the world" and employee-centric culture.

COST ISSUES

Cost can significantly influence the design of a rewards program. Costs come in many varieties:

- **Time**—related to the costs of using the people involved in the design, review, and approval of the program
- **Implementation**—includes the administrative costs of the program as well as the costs relating to the communication of the program to employees

- **Funding**—includes any plan contributions or premiums. Funding issues may also include trust fund establishment and maintenance
- **Compliance**—consists of costs related to meeting federal or local regulations
- **Budgeting**—decides the total amount of funding available to the rewards program. This also includes the parameters for various items inside the program
- **Support staff**—includes the personnel needed to effectively establish and administer the compensation program

Budgeting considerations affect the guidelines for base pay and benefits. The pay structure establishes the parameters for the salary costs of jobs within the company. Salary ranges provide additional guidance for individual compensation decisions. Benefit programs, according to the Department of Labor, typically add about 40 percent to the total payroll cost. Benefit programs are rising in costs due to increasing healthcare costs. Benefit costs are also affected by demographic shifts.

Cost-control efforts involve proper adjustments of compensation and benefits. Compensation is adjusted to reflect the current or market pay rate. Costs associated with compensation can also be computed to predict future costs. Benefit offerings are often adjusted for the best mix of cost and employee value. Sourcing of benefits, which is evaluating the costs of several benefit vendors, is the most important cost control for benefit management.

WHAT IS THE TOTAL REWARDS DESIGN PROCESS?

The intent of a rewards package is to promote employee behavior that will accomplish and become aligned with organizational goals. Before building a rewards package, the company must define specific achievements to target. In addition, there should be a smooth, well thought-out process that positions one for success. (Figure 3-1)

Figure 3-1.

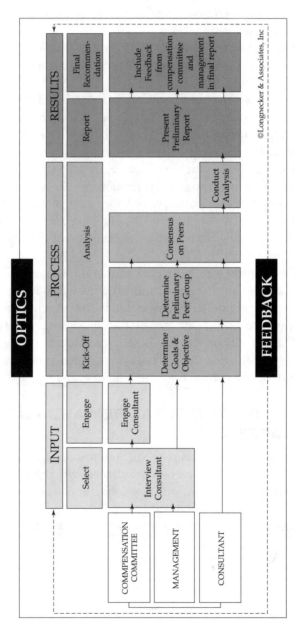

©Longnecker & Associates, Inc

PHILOSOPHY, MISSION, AND STRATEGY

The first step of the design process is to evaluate the corporate strategy. The strategy of a company is actually a product of the company's philosophy and mission. These elements are set by the ownership and upper management of the organization.

DEFINITION

An organizational philosophy is the often informal set of beliefs and values that provide the core essence of the organization. The purpose of the philosophy is to provide a guideline for how the company approaches business.

Spawned from the corporate philosophy is the mission statement. This is a formalized pronouncement of what the organization is about, what is important, and how it approaches the world. Mission statements are used by management to display organizational direction.

The typical mission statement identifies the stakeholders of the company that might include customer/clients, vendors, employees, and shareholders/owners. It answers the questions: What is our business? Why do we exist? Where are we headed? Additionally, it may detail the market space or product. This example of a mission statement combines these elements with a plan for how the company is going to accomplish the broad goals:

> *Our goal is to become the supplier of choice to the home improvement industry. By supplying top quality products, delivering excellent customer service and working in partnership with our customers to satisfy their needs, we aim to be the best. As we see it, that's the best way we can properly serve the long-term interests of all our constituents: customers, suppliers, employees and stockholders.*
>
> —Ply Gem Industries, Inc.

The business strategy is the actual plan for achieving the mission while following corporate philosophy. Strategy is the broad scheme for positioning the company's products and services in a way that accomplishes the mission. The development of the strategic plan is usually more involved than defining the philosophy and mission because the strategy must cope with a greater set of variables. The strategy must also be checked for consistency with the corporate philosophy and mission statement.

Many different elements converge to form the business strategy, which is why the construction of the plan requires a cross-functional team. Some of the elements of a business strategy may include:

- Pricing
- Quality
- Innovation
- Research and Development
- Service
- Adaptability
- Finance
- Product or Service Differentiation
- Rate of Return
- Costs
- Target Market
- Sales Structure
- Marketing Techniques
- Production Methods
- Product
- Logistics

Research indicates a strong correlation between organizational performance and mission statements that define purpose, values, behavioral standards, intent to satisfy stakeholder groups, and competitive strategy.

Typically, a company decides which elements are critical to the successful pursuit of the mission statement. For example, a network integrator may focus on providing cutting-edge technologies (innovation) with high availability (quality) and high value (rate of return) for the customer.

The strategy of an organization sets the tone for the rest of the organizational design. The elements of the design must align with the rest of the organization. Human Resources can act as a major reinforcement for this alignment by attracting, retaining, and motivating talent that supports the requirements of the corporate strategy. Therefore, the next step to reward system design is the development of a human resource philosophy.

BEST PRACTICE

Dealing with change

Company name:	HCC Corporation
Problem faced by company:	Due to industry changes, HCC was facing many dramatic changes in its organizational mission, structure, and composition which was leading to a misunderstanding of corporate goals. The result was high turnover and low productivity.
Compensation solutions:	HCC first redefined the company's new goals and strategies. HR programs could then be destroyed or redesigned in support of the company's new direction. During this process, it was evident that some positions would need to be eliminated. A career transition program was created to assist those employees who were being transitioned out. The program provided for severance and career counseling. For those employees who were to remain with HCC, a change management program was implemented, which focused on job education and job progression.
Benefit to company:	Employees understood the mission and changes encompassing HCC and worked diligently to ensure HCC was positioned for the future. In addition, those employees who were transitioned out were treated with dignity, maintaining HCC's excellent public image.

HUMAN RESOURCE PHILOSOPHY AND STRATEGY

As with the overall corporate strategy, the human resource strategy begins with a philosophy. The philosophy toward human resources consists of the values and beliefs applied by management toward its relationships with employees. The human resources philosophy and the overall business strategy are used to synthesize a human resources strategy.

The human resource strategy is the plan to gather, keep, and inspire talent. This plan is the set of broad guidelines that includes the rewards package, "customer (employee) service," and other initiatives. The largest element of human resource strategy is the rewards package that leads to the development of a total rewards philosophy.

TOTAL REWARDS PHILOSOPHY

The organizational approach to developing the rewards philosophy must include a macro view of the programs, the culture, the employees, and the structure of the organization. In order to build this view, the following questions must be answered as completely and as expansively as possible.

What is the company culture and environment?

As discussed earlier, each organization has its own unique culture. Any total rewards initiative must be in line with the current culture unless the intent is to transform the current culture. Obviously, in the event of a culture change, the rewards system should work with other change agents to assist the culture shift.

The corporate environment and morale are also important to the design of a rewards philosophy. The rewards philosophy must encourage employees to stay motivated when times are difficult. When the outlook for the company is good, the philosophy should work toward continuing the positive outlook.

What must the company do to attract, retain, and motivate employees?

The reward package must be designed in a manner that attracts, retains, and motivates the exact type of employee that would fit the corporate culture. Not only must the company understand the employees and potential employees, but it must also understand external factors that might motivate people to act in certain ways. The company must be able to respond to these factors in a manner that is appealing to employees and potential employees.

What are the objectives?

The three primary objectives are attraction, retention, and motivation. Different elements of reward strategies target different goals. Objectives can be broad or focused. The broad objectives are more appropriately part of the philosophy. More focused objectives will shape actual reward package design.

What is the role of human resources?

The function of human resources in the organization must be defined. This definition will allow the human resources department to set priorities and decide where to focus resources. Any or all of the following are typical roles:

- Filling open positions
- Reducing employee turnover
- Promoting performance
- Reinforcing corporate culture
- Serving operations
- Developing employees
- Improving relations among employees
- Communicating vision

What are the performance goals?

As with the other questions, this knowledge is important in structuring the rewards package. Motivational rewards are more effective when they align directly with the goals of the organization. Also, a strong understanding of the performance goals is necessary to build an appropriate method of measuring progress toward earning rewards. Performance goals may range from company-wide goals to individual goals. Other performance goals may be for the program itself.

What are the cost constraints?

A cost analysis of potential rewards options is necessary in order to ensure that the actual rewards package has a positive net effect on the bottom line. During the examination of costs, HR should design a methodology of measuring the rewards system against the financial performance of the company. The budget for the rewards system should also be set during this part of the evaluation.

At this point, a total rewards philosophy statement should evolve out of the process of answering these key questions.

TOTAL REWARDS PHILOSOPHY STATEMENT

Management should express its values and beliefs about total rewards through a total rewards philosophy statement. The total rewards philosophy statement serves several purposes within the organization:

- The statement guides the development of reward plans.
- Corporate culture and strategy are reinforced.
- Management states expectations and commitments to employees.
- The statement is a measuring stick for reward plans.

The total rewards statement should be broadcast frequently to the employees. Care should be taken to make sure employees actually understand the intents and views of management. Employees should also have the opportunity to provide feedback and clarify their understanding.

COMPONENTS OF THE TOTAL REWARDS PHILOSOPHY STATEMENT

A total reward philosophy statement has several key components. These components should clarify for both management and employees the intents and standard practices associated with the program.

Objectives

The objectives of the rewards philosophy should detail the reason the company is developing this philosophy along with specific business goals. This reinforcement of the business strategy assists employees in an effort to understand the relationship between organizational and personal success.

Desired competitive position

By stating the desired competitive position, companies detail how they approach the labor market. Typically, companies determine their desired position as a percentile of the market value of the rewards package. The market is usually defined as industry competitors. Program element values are easier to determine if this section is specific.

Values regarding internal equity

With these values, companies communicate various aspects of how packages are assigned. Job factors that affect compensation are outlined. Also, the correlations between pay and performance and pay and tenure should be detailed.

Values regarding communications

Companies should state how often they will discuss the rewards program with employees. They should also explain how open the communication about the plan will be.

Values regarding benefits cost sharing

The rewards philosophy statement provides an outline of the distribution of costs related to any benefits. Employees need to have an understanding of any benefits that may require an employee contribution.

Desired mix

The preferred mix of reward elements should be outlined in the reward philosophy statement. These elements include base pay, short- and long-term incentives, benefits, perquisites, and work experience. The mix will depend heavily on the goals and culture of the organization.

These components are typically used to craft a rewards statement similar to this example.

BEST PRACTICE

XYZ Corporation Rewards philosophy statement

As a professional services firm operating in a highly competitive environment, we at XYZ Corporation recognize that people are our primary asset and our principal source of competitive advantage. To achieve our financial objectives, we must attract, retain, and motivate a highly qualified and competent work force. Accordingly, our base pay will be targeted at the 75th percentile of the professional services sector, while remaining internally equitable.

We will utilize performance-based incentive programs to supplement our base pay such that average direct compensation will approximate the 90th percentile of cash compensation versus our defined competitor group when our overall financial performance meets or exceeds target.

Additionally, equity (partnership) participation will be extended to the top five percent of our professional staff, as determined by our partner/principal selection process.

In addition to cash compensation opportunities, XYZ Corporation will provide a comprehensive benefits program addressing our employees' health and welfare, income security, and capital accumulation needs/concerns. All programs will be contributory in nature and designed in a flexible manner to enable employees to select the coverage most consistent with their needs and circumstances. Profit sharing contributions by XYZ Corporation to its retirement savings plan will be contingent upon the achievement of all established financial targets.

XYZ Corporation values the components of the work experience, including a positive and healthy work environment that addresses the physical and emotional well-being of employees and their families. Components enhancing the employees' work experience will be consistent with the offerings by Fortune Magazine's "100 Best Companies to Work For." All total rewards programs will be communicated to employees on a regular basis.

Total rewards expenditures shall not exceed 60 percent of XYZ Corporation's annual revenues, including statutorily required contributions for FICA, unemployment compensation, and workers' compensation.

Rewards statements can be fairly brief like this one, but many are much longer. Some may take several pages to also explain many of the rewards initiatives in detail. Some might have a statement that discusses the core values and beliefs of the company about its workforce. The statement then details the elements of the total rewards package, which clarifies the complete intent of the rewards program.

PUTTING THE REWARDS PACKAGE TOGETHER

The next step of the design process is to actually put the elements into a rewards package. This is done within the parameters defined during the previous steps. Remember that each package should be individualized to maximize its effectiveness. All packages should be checked for consistency to ensure fair reward plans are established throughout the organization.

BUILDING A PROGRAM

Developing a program is straight forward because the process consists of fairly intuitive subroutines. These are:

- Define the objective
- Determine eligibility
- Select elements and build the framework
- Determine funding
- Define measurements
- Develop a course of action
- Clear the plan with senior management - *SHOULD BE FIRST*

#1

Program development begins with defining the objective or purpose to explain why the program is necessary. This process should also lead to the clarification of the principles and objectives of the program which can then be communicated to both employees and senior management. For example, a common objective is "to improve customer service."

After the objective is designed, program eligibility must be determined. Since each program is different, companies must determine which employees need to be part of the program in order to positively impact the company. This step can be treacherous, because a failure to clearly justify the decision could risk alienating non-eligible groups inside the company. This phase of the development process should result in a clearly established set of eligibility criteria.

At this point in the design process, the elements of the total reward package that are most valued by the eligible employees must be identified. The mix should be tested and evaluated for efficiency with the assistance of the affected employees. The actual elements themselves should be linked to the desired business goals during this phase and checked for alignment. Next, communicate to the eligible group the types of behaviors the rewards program is meant to encourage. This communication should also include feedback to allow further focusing of the program design and to promote employee understanding.

Throughout the three previous steps, the evaluation of funding must take place. During this part of the process, sources of funding must be tapped and costs must be analyzed. Different components of the rewards program may have different funding requirements and opportunities. Typically, the biggest concern is cost. The constant estimation of program costs reduces the possibilities of unforeseen adverse financial effects on the company due to new rewards initiatives. Good strategies for anticipating costs and funding requirements include:

- Developing an estimate for each component of the rewards regime
- Outlining parameters
- Identifying potential problem areas
- Undertaking a cost/benefit analysis
- Searching out funding options
- Investigating potential tax situations (good and bad)
- Evaluating legal ramifications

All of these efforts can assist in the development of a sound funding strategy for a new rewards program.

METRICS

To achieve the most benefit, a company's rewards program must be measurable. The key to measuring the success or failure of a rewards program rests primarily in the design of the measurement tools.

Good measurement tools should have the following characteristics:

- Successful accomplishment of objectives should be apparent.
- Metrics should be overt and straight forward.
- Outside influences should not affect results.
- Accuracy and veracity should be easily proven.
- Participants should be able to have complete comprehension of measurements.
- Cause and effect relationships between the participants and outcomes should be determinable.

Well-designed metrics can assist the company in the evaluation of employees in order to assign rewards and to identify areas of potential growth.

After developing the schemes associated with the previous pieces of program development, a course of action must be decided. This is the actual project planning of the implementation phase. Several organizational factors go into the development of this timeline. Corporate culture and the organizational propensity for change are the two factors that can most affect the pace and aggressiveness of the implementation schedule. Time must be allotted for planning activities, seeking approval, testing, and communicating the program to employees and management. A review program should also be included in the implementation schedule to assure that the program will be thoroughly evaluated. As human resources departments are often understaffed, the implementation plans of various programs should be prioritized for maximum effect.

The approval of senior management is mandatory before the actual implementation of a new rewards initiative occurs. Schedule time for management approval within the implementation timeline. Senior management may require evidence of need and benefit. Therefore, be prepared to demonstrate the program's effect on the bottom line and how the program correlates with the company's strategies and goals.

EVALUATION

Now that the total rewards design process has been explained, the time has come to evaluate the current rewards system. On the first evaluation pass, it is important to gain an understanding about the current system. Deliberate calls for change are not necessary during the first examination. Any faults found in the total rewards scheme will implicitly cause evaluators to ask, "If what we've got is wrong, what would be right?"

As explained in the design process, the first step to approaching a rewards system is to review the corporate philosophy, mission, and strategy. If these three items are not consistent with each other, then this discrepancy must be understood and corrected before proceeding with the evaluation.

The correction of a disjoint between the corporate strategy, mission, and philosophy will require a concerted effort on the part of management. Management may not believe that correcting this disjoint is imperative, but for the designer of a rewards program, the alignment of these three key pieces is mandatory. Without clarification, unintentional mistakes may be made which serve to either reduce production, increase costs, or both.

After confirming the alignment of the overall corporate drivers, the rewards design planners must decide how the human resources philosophy and strategy work to support the corporate strategy. The two must be evaluated in terms of each to ensure they are both trying to achieve the same goals. If the human resources philosophy and strategy are not aligned with corporate strategy, then the decision makers in human resources must rebuild the two in a manner that best supports corporate strategy.

Now that all of the upstream issues are in alignment, the total rewards philosophy can be examined. As this is the focal item for the total reward system designer, this examination needs to be exhaustive. Every element should be brought to light and examined for relevance and purpose.

EXAMINING THE PHILOSOPHY

As the design team evaluates the total rewards philosophy, it must ask many questions in order to establish the correlation between the philosophy and corporate goals. During its examination of the philosophy, the designers must understand issues such as:

- **Compliance.** Does the philosophy provide the mechanisms to meet both the letter and the intent of any regulatory statutes?
- **Processes.** Are processes in place to support the implementation of the philosophy and its related rewards plans?
- **Employees.** Do the employees understand the philosophy, including the intents and implementation?
- **Management.** Does management support the philosophy? Does management understand how to appropriately use it?
- **Components.** What are the components of the philosophy? How do they work together to make the philosophy work?
- **Measurements.** How is the philosophy performance to be measured? How are individual elements to be judged for success?

Other questions that may be used to expand the evaluation of the total rewards philosophy may be found in the Internal Audit at the end of this chapter.

If some of the answers to these types of questions are not clear or not satisfying, the philosophy may need adjusting. If the philosophy needs a complete overhaul, the answers to most questions during the examination will be negative. Obviously, if problems occur at this stage, then they must be resolved before continuing through the evaluation.

WHAT'S IN THE PACKAGE

Assuming the examination of the philosophy did not lead to any consternation, the next step of the evaluation is to look at the actual rewards packages. Because of the variety of packages involved, the different types of packages need to be defined and job definitions need to be detailed. After being designated, the rewards packages and the jobs need to be matched together.

Before evaluating the actual reward package for each job, the goals of the reward package need to be defined. In some cases, this may be a tactical decision based on the immediate needs of the company. The goals of a mature company with an aging workforce will probably differ from those of a rapidly growing startup.

Once the goals are established, the components of the rewards package should be evaluated. As Chapter One detailed, each element has a different purpose in the total rewards package. As a reminder, the purpose of each component is as follows:

- **Base pay**—sets the minimum value of the particular job for the company and provides a baseline standard of living for the employee. The base pay is a key ingredient in the initial attraction of new employees.
- **Short-term incentives**—are awarded as a result of performance. Employees use these to enhance their current standards of living. Short-term incentives are primarily used to motivate employees.
- **Long-term incentives**—are awarded for performance over time. These are often used by employees to build wealth. Because these often have employment requirements, long-term incentives are used mostly to retain employees.
- **Benefits**—provide security for employees and are used to attract and retain employees.
- **Perquisites**—provide "psychic income" for employees. Perquisites can assist in the attraction, retention, and motivation of employees.
- **Work experience**—leads to job satisfaction and employment. This also can work to attract, retain, and motivate employees.

The intent of each of these components should be outlined for each type of rewards package. By identifying how the elements work together, the actual package alignment with the goals of the human resource strategy can be verified—whether the strategy is to fuel workforce expansion, reduce turnover, or boost production.

METRICS

As one of the intents of a total rewards system is to increase employee output, the performance metrics for each job should be identified. After isolating each metric, the metric should be studied for effectiveness. The effectiveness of each metric is a direct result of its alignment with the corporate goals. The appropriateness as a measurement for that particular job should be taken into account. For example, the janitor should be measured by the cleanliness of the office and not by the performance of a mutual fund run from the office.

After a thorough evaluation, the total rewards program will require fixing, development, or maintenance:

- The program will need to be fixed if it exists but has flaws.
- Development is required if no comprehensive rewards program exists. (Most companies have a rewards program, but some have atrophied).
- If the total rewards program is sound, then all that needs to be done is periodic maintenance to prevent the obsolescence of any program elements.

Often, the appropriate next steps can be identified through conversations with management and the employees. Of course, other information is almost always required to make improvement.

A program in need of an overhaul can be identified through expressed attitudes such as:

- "The company will always take care of the employees,"—which implies that the employees view the rewards program as an entitlement.
- "We set aside a $400 million dollar compensation and benefits package,"—management may not be in touch with what its actual employees want and just states an impressive dollar amount.

Typically, management and employees are complacent with their views of the compensation interactions. Human resources in general and the total rewards evaluation team in particular must convince both management and employees that the rewards system can make the work relationship more fulfilling for both parties.

The system overhaul can be of two different varieties—the "fixer-upper" or "re-do."

The "Fixer-Upper"

So, the program is not perfect. If copious notes were taken during the evaluation, deciding where to start will be easy. Identify the weaknesses in the rewards program first. Before changing anything, a cost benefit analysis should be run at the points of contention in order to discover whether the potential impact is worth the effort of fixing.

If fixing the problem makes financial sense, then find the issue closest to the corporate mission statement and strategy. The best way to approach the repair of a total rewards system is to start on a macro view and work toward the more detailed aspects. The actual total reward design process may be used to guide the progression from the macro view to the micro perspective. This process is described earlier in this chapter.

Fixing the total rewards design can be difficult at times. Management must be aware of and supportive of the proposed changes. Care must be taken to ensure that employees are aware of and understand the changes. New initiatives must be checked against residual ones to determine efficacy. Plan administrators often get stretched during the adjustment process.

"Re-Do"

If fixing a few things here and there won't salvage the plan (or lack of one), then it is time to start over. Having to start over is not always a bad thing because opportunities to do things the right way abound. The process is the same as the guidelines for developing a total rewards design process.

Starting over requires even more management support than fixing the process because the total rewards program may need to be totally different than anything the company has ever used.

TOOLS USED IN THE EVALUATION OF A TOTAL REWARDS PROGRAM

Many different tools and measurements can be used to evaluate total rewards strategies. The evaluation of a total rewards program requires both quantitative and qualitative techniques. Some of the tools evaluate programs in terms of costs. Others evaluate the effects of initiatives on production. Still others evaluate direct human resources results.

Financial and accounting tools and measurements

Financial tools and measurements are usually used to evaluate the performance of the company, the costs related to total rewards programs, and other "big picture" perspectives. All financial ratios and measurements should be used with predefined comparisons, and in conjunction with other tools, to create the best possible view of overall performance in order to properly assign rewards and incentives.

Financial measurements are most relevant to any broadly assigned company-wide incentives, executive incentives, and evaluations of the reward system itself.

Return on Assets (ROA) is a measure of a company's performance relative to the assets of the company. Financial companies and other companies with large amounts of capital often use this measurement:

Return on Assets = Net Income/Total Assets

Return on Equity (ROE) is used by most other companies as a measure of performance relative to the stockholders' actual stake in the company. ROE fails to account for the outstanding debt of a company.

Return on Equity = Net Income/Total Shareholders' Equity

Return on Total Capital (ROTC) is used in the same context as ROE. However, ROTC factors out long-term debt to provide a clearer picture of the ROE without the bias caused by debt structure.

Return on Total Capital = (Net Income + Interest on Long Term Debt)/ (Shareholders' Equity + Long Term Debt)

Earnings per Share (EPS) are a measure of a company's performance in relationship to outstanding shares. EPS is similar to ROE with different limitations. EPS does not take into account the dilutive effects of convertible bonds, stock options, and warrants.

Earnings per Share = Net Income/Average Shares Outstanding

Return on Sales (ROS) can be interpreted as a measure of efficiency. This ratio isolates the percentage of sales that does not go to paying any overhead or other costs (except perhaps debt service). This indicator is often used by manufacturing and service companies to evaluate organizational efficiency.

Return on Sales = Net Income/Net Sales

OPERATIONS TOOLS AND MEASUREMENTS

Individual rewards and incentives are often based on operational efficiency. Therefore, the knowledge of a few simple formulas can be of great assistance for human resource professionals.

Throughput or Flow Rate is a measure of productivity based on number of units processed in a given amount of time. This may be used for order processing or installation of a circuit board. The concept is the same whether the actual product is a service or a manufactured good.

Throughput = number of units/time

Cycle Time can be used as another method to measure productivity. Cycle time is the amount of time it takes to complete a unit of the business process or work activity.

Inventory is not typically used directly. But it allows for the computation of other indicators of operation efficiency.

Inventory = Throughput X Cycle Time (Little's Law)

Turnover indicates how efficiently resources are being used. High turnover means that the organization is potentially getting more return for its resources (except for when turnover refers to the labor force). Turnover can be computed two different ways from the previously mentioned operational measurements.

Turnover = Throughput/Inventory or 1/Cycle Time

Task Time can be used similarly to cycle time as a team measurement. Task time is the average time between completions of a task, so it only differs from cycle time if more than one operator is working on the same identical task.

Other operational ratios and indicators may be used as performance measures, as well. Some of the categories may include quality control, logistics, and customer service. Quality control could be measured by using a ratio of defects to total units. Logistics functions could be measured using delivery time or price measures.

HUMAN RESOURCE TOOLS AND MEASUREMENTS

Some of the principles of operations and finance can serve as the foundations for human resource specific measurements. These measurements can serve to associate costs and cost savings with human resource activities.

Employee Turnover is a measure of the efficiency and effectiveness of the attraction and retention initiatives. Employee turnover is calculated the same way that inventory turnover is calculated. This measurement is important because of the costs associated with training new hires.

Employee Turnover = 1/Average Length of Employment

From the employee turnover rate, the cost of turnover can be calculated. This allows for the computation of the return on investment of a new rewards initiative. Not only can this be used as an estimate, but the return on investment calculation can also be used to review the actual impact of a new program.

Turnover Cost = Average Salary X # of employees X Turnover Rate

A typical ROI comparison may be look like the following table.

Table 3-A

Company Size	25% Turnover Rate	15% Turnover Rate
50	$500,000	$300,000
500	$5,000,000	$3,000,000
5000	$50,000,000	$30,000,000

(assuming average salary is $40,000)

As the table shows, a substantial savings is available to companies that can reduce turnover—which is the same as increasing retention. The importance of this savings becomes more apparent as the size of the company increases. Through calculations such as this, the true value of a strong total rewards program can be computed.

Other qualitative methods such as questionnaires, personal interviews, and feedback sessions can be used to measure the success of a rewards program. These types of evaluations can be used to pinpoint desires of employees and the pros and cons of a rewards system in a way that can not always be evaluated by a quantitative system. Technology has made employee involvement with total rewards systems easier and has made the overall effectiveness of the system more measurable.

BEST PRACTICE

An example of the use of technology in total rewards systems comes from HayGroup's implementation of a "My Total Rewards" site for Avaya. Not only did this site add functionality and transparency for the employees of Avaya, but it also generated more interest in the rewards program itself. The feedback and comments generated by the employees enabled the human resources department to have a better understanding of the future needs and current successes of the rewards system.

Some of the comments generated from employees included:

"Great work—this is so very cool! Easy to follow, easy to drill down. And I believe it effectively makes the point regarding the investment Avaya makes in each employee."

And

"I would like to compliment Avaya on providing this very useful snapshot of our individual benefits. So often in the past, I (and I am sure many others) have been frustrated in having to look for this information in so many different places. The presentation of the information is very organized and user friendly."

This type of feedback not only is useful as far as identifying the employees' needs, but it also serves as a reward for the planning and implementation team.

The internal HR audit below is a tool that will lead human resource personnel through the discovery and thought processes of a total rewards system. Each question should be answered to identify strengths and weaknesses of the current total reward philosophy, strategy, and programs.

HR AUDIT

COMPENSATION ADMINISTRATION

- Do your practices comply with FLSA regulations?
- Have you performed a periodic review and audit of practices and processes?
- Is an HRIS system in place that ensures ongoing data integrity?
- Are all remuneration policies fully documented and established?
- Are established processes adhered to?
- Is a job evaluation system in place that distinguishes between jobs?
- Does a compensation philosophy exist, in writing, that addresses:
  - Which geographic and industry markets are used for benchmarks?
  - How pay is set in relation to the benchmarks?
- What is the balance between internal and external equity?

DIRECT COMPENSATION

- Does the incentive system drive performance rather than just serving as a bonus?
- Are solid performance and process measures in place?
- Are pay practices non-discriminatory?
- Is there an effective balance between base and variable pay?
- Are hourly pay practices in compliance with any contractual obligations?

INDIRECT COMPENSATION

- Are time and effort spent in communicating pertinent information about the value of benefits?
- Do employees understand their benefits?
- Does the organization have managed care insurance systems fully in place?

- Is a co-pay approach in existence and is it set at the correct amount?
- Are benefits in line with industry practice?
- Are retirement savings plans properly funded?
- Is the employee benefits design compatible with the demographics and business conditions of the organization?
- Are plan qualifications being adhered to?
- Are legally required plan documents being issued consistent with applicable laws?
- Does a process exist to resolve benefits maintenance issues?
- Are benefits programs evaluated to remain cost-effective for the business?

PERFORMANCE APPRAISAL

- Does the performance management process align with the business strategy and total compensation philosophy?
- Does a performance management process exist that focuses on linking employees' skills, contributions, and career needs with the needs of the business?
- Does the performance management process include developmental plans?
- Is an assessment system in place for hourly employees?
- Does the policy state that each employee is entitled to a formal performance appraisal at least once a year?
- Is the basis of performance appraisals the formal, written job descriptions for the job being performed and agreed-upon performance improvement items from previous performance appraisals?
- Will the performance appraisal be affected by race, sex, religion, national origin, age, handicap, or status as a veteran?
- Will employees have a right to appeal an unsatisfactory performance appraisal to a neutral party within the company?
- Can employees include their own written performance appraisal comments in their files upon request?
- Do supervisors have to obtain an employee signature on the performance appraisal document to indicate that the performance appraisal has been discussed with the employee?
- Are all supervisors trained in performance appraisal techniques within six months after receiving their first supervisory assignment and every three years thereafter?

COMPETITIVE PAY LEVELS

- Are pay structure control points at the desired competitive pay level—consistently at all points in the structure?
- Is the survey base relevant for the location/industry/jobs?
- Is there unexplained turnover in any job families or categories?
- Is there compression between supervisor and non-supervisors or between new hires and more experienced people on the same job?
- Are there different competitive pay objectives for any special job categories? How are they implemented?
- What is communicated to employees about the competitiveness of their pay? Is it attainable?
- Has the merit budgeting in recent periods been targeted at problem areas?
- Does actual pay follow competitive objectives consistently?
- Are employees under the merit plan being paid for performance or other factors such as seniority?
- Is the merit pay program adversely affecting protected class employees?
- Do employees perceive that their pay is based on performance?
- Are exceptions documented and based on business necessity?

COMMUNICATIONS

- What is communicated to all employees?
- Do employees receive consistent information?
- Do supervisors and managers understand their responsibility to communicate?
- Do employees understand the pay system and its elements?
- What are employee expectations about their pay?

JOB EVALUATION PLANS

- Do the factors represent all major content aspects of jobs found in the company?
- Do the factors represent the skills, effort, responsibilities, and working conditions that the company management wishes to pay for?
- Do factor weightings reflect business necessity?
- Are degrees of each factor scaled and defined properly and in the full range of each degree used?
- How does each factor affect male vs. female dominated jobs?

- Is inter-rater reliability at acceptable levels? For each factor? For the plan as a whole?
- If the plan results are different than market reality, how are the differences reconciled?
- Is administration consistent?
- Do managers, supervisors, and employees understand the job evaluation plan? Do they know how to appeal a job evaluation decision?
- Are reliable results being achieved by the plan? In other words, do different job evaluators achieve the same results with the plan?
- Do the factor definitions fit the jobs in the work environment?
- Is more than one plan in use? If so, are any jobs adversely affected?
- Does the plan provide a consistent link to pay in the labor market?

JOB DOCUMENTATION

- Does the job documentation provide adequate information to support the job evaluation system?
- Is job documentation accurate, complete, and up-to-date?
- Are skill, knowledge, and experience criteria job-related and realistic?
- Was job documentation developed with input from immediate supervision or job incumbents?
- Is job documentation adequate to support the other purposes for which it may be used—performance appraisal, training, employment, etc.?

From this audit, the compensation team should be able to generate new opportunities and ideas within the total rewards framework for how to better align rewards programs with the external and internal needs and goals of the corporation.

CHAPTER FOUR

CONNECTING YOUR CORPORATE CULTURE AND COMPENSATION

OBJECTIVE

The corporate culture "fit" is an important criteria in developing the available talent of a company. Culture is an important factor in employment and retention. In order for a company to attract and retain top talent, that talent must be comfortable with the people around them and share common beliefs including the direction of the company.

KEY POINTS

◊ Corporate culture can, if used properly, lead to better performance.
◊ Corporate culture is influenced by the compensation plan.
◊ The way a company rewards its employees is a strong indicator of corporate values and beliefs.
◊ The most important way to connect the compensation plan to the organizational plan is through well-organized communication.

So far, compensation strategies have been the focal points of discussion. Now, reasons behind the importance of compensation strategy design need to be brought to light. Compensation design is important because of its potential for significant impact on corporate culture.

WHAT IS CORPORATE CULTURE?

"... the collection of values, beliefs, symbols and norms that the organization follows and that define what it is and how it does business each and every day."

—Peter P. Fornal

Corporate culture can be described in the same fashion as regional or national cultures. Quite simply, culture is the collection of beliefs and values as demonstrated through common actions, rituals, and symbols and passed from one generation to the next.

DEFINITION

In the *American Heritage Dictionary*, culture is defined as "the predominating attitudes and behavior that characterize the functioning of a group or organization."

Culture can help individuals identify appropriate behavioral patterns. Culture also plays an important role in communicating the values of a company to outsiders. It is the window through which people view the organization. This statement applies to individuals within the organization as well. In the business context, culture was previously defined as "the shared beliefs and values of the members of an organization." The implications of culture are being refined in today's business lexicon.

HOW DOES CULTURE AFFECT AN ORGANIZATION?

Corporate culture shapes expectations and influences how people go about their business, adapt to situations, and learn. Corporate culture can also shape habits and roles. By shaping the roles and habits of individuals, corporate culture can influence styles of thinking, acting, and communicating to meet the expectations of the group. This influence can, if used properly in the correct context, lead to better performance.

What influences corporate culture?

Corporate culture is influenced by management. This influence is primarily exerted through management behavior, not through the issuance of edicts (although these sometimes allow employees to have an idea of what management is thinking.) In the last several years, we have seen many examples of corporate culture dysfunction due to excessive behavior of management, namely, at companies such as Enron, WorldCom, and Tyco. However, corporate culture can be influenced in both directions, and many successful organizations have strong corporate cultures with management teams that display the appropriate cultural values everyday.

Corporate culture is also influenced by the compensation plan. The way a company rewards its employees is a strong indicator of corporate values and beliefs. The correlation between rewards and values can range across compensation strategies:

- Heavy use of stock options would imply a belief in company growth.
- Reimbursement for education would show an emphasis on personal growth.
- Paid childcare emphasizes the value of family.

These examples are just a few of the ways that the compensation package can underscore the corporate culture.

The other key piece of attraction and retention is the strategy on how organizations compensate their employees. This strategy must work with the culture for mutual reinforcement.

ESTABLISHING A COMPENSATION STRATEGY THAT FITS YOUR COMPANY

Imitation is the greatest form of flattery—and is evidenced in many ways—from the defensive trends of the National Football League to the abundance of self-help books. Compensation is no different. Everyone is looking for the magic package. What if the secret is even simpler than a magic formula?

Why does a compensation program that is an extraordinary success at one company fail to meet expectations at another? Companies are different—they have different cultures, needs, and expectations—and because they are different, the incredibly successful compensation plan at Company A could very well be a recipe for disaster at Company B.

The important thing is to understand how and why each individual idea works in a particular company. Tailoring successful ideas allows the compensation design team to draw from an extremely large toolbox.

The most important part of a compensation program is the structure. With a larger collection of tools comes a greater amount of flexibility. This flexibility increases the likelihood of compensation plan success.

Successful compensation strategies begin with an assessment of the present or desired corporate culture. Is the purpose of the new compensation strategy to reinforce or shift the corporate culture? The understanding of the desired culture and the intent of the compensation strategy allow management to better link the compensation strategy to workplace performance of employees.

> *Compensation is key to uncovering an organization's hidden personality. That personality is uncovered by the outcome (the performance and behavior of employees) of a compensation strategy that has been recently implemented.*
>
> —Craig Cantoni

How is corporate culture assessed? Corporate cultures are made of a variety of elements that can be defined through several models. Thomas Flannery, David Hofrichter, and Paul Platte have outlined four distinct cultural models: the Functional Culture Model; the Process Model; the Time-Based Model; and the Network Model.

Functional Culture Model (traditional culture)

This model is the traditional model in use today. Companies under this model focus on consistency. The primary driver is the need to accumulate applied technology resources. Corporate risk is limited through reliable production. Departmental interaction is in the form of handoffs as work is done sequentially as opposed to interactively.

Because of the separation of departments and responsibilities, most systems involve hierarchy and are control oriented. Performance measures are also traditional—size, industry reputation, and return on equity. This culture is effective in industries and companies where a high degree of reliability is crucial.

Compensation strategies for the functional model are also somewhat traditional. Individual values are emphasized. Rewards are not typically based on team achievements. The primary component of pay is the base salary. Base salary is established by a pay grade system. Promotion from one pay grade to another occurs through the development of strictly defined skills. High performance is rewarded by promotion through the hierarchy. This usually occurs via a new job title, increased responsibility, or both. Often, a merit pay increase coincides with the promotion.

Process Model: service and quality

The Process Model is growing in popularity, especially in service-based industries. Work in a process environment is designed around processes for meeting obligations to customers. The corporate focus is on continually improving the quality of customer interactions and of the goods and services provided. Companies with a process culture strive to achieve optimal customer satisfaction. In the pursuit of customer satisfaction, employees are often required to cooperate, plan, execute, and solve problems directly with the customer. Teamwork, both internal and external, is a vital part of the process culture.

Compensation strategies for process cultures revolve around teamwork and customer satisfaction. Employees are expected to build team skills and relationships as well as individual skills. Compensation levels are often dictated by team competencies. Variable pay is more prevalent to encourage alignment with quality and customer service goals. Performance assessments often involve multi-rater systems (from peers, managers, subordinates, and customers). All employees are expected to take at least some responsibility for the company's performance. Effective incentive plans in a process-driven organization balance the measurement of company-wide goals with the methods of achieving those goals. As such, gain-sharing programs are often successful.

Time-Based Model: speed and agility

The Time-Based cultural Model is also increasing in importance as the rate of change in the world increases. Because the products of many of the companies with this model have short life cycles, the corporate emphasis is on speed and cost of capital. The fierce competition in the typical industry sectors of these companies requires companies to anticipate and create demand, and even create new markets, in order to succeed. The constant requirement to push the envelope forces companies in this market space to depend on research and development teams and task forces to continually find new opportunities and improvements. Corporate performance is measured by economic value added and market share.

Compensation and business strategies for time-based cultures are constructed around current initiatives rather than extended time-frames. The skill and competencies of both individuals and teams are stressed. This is done through the acknowledgement (and expectation) of significant breakthroughs which carry more value and weight than constant gradual improvement. The value of an employee is based on the contribution to the overall effort, not the position or title. Professional growth through achieving new competencies takes the place of vertical "up the career ladder" growth. Base salary tends to be below market rate, but incentive pay is widespread and substantial. Variable pay is often used to link compensation directly with the results on individual or group projects. Increases are paid out through incentives (both short-term and long-term) rather than additional base pay. Typically, all employees are involved in long-term incentive programs. The structure of the strategies of companies with time-based cultures is designed to provide maximum flexibility and maneuverability.

Network Model: "Virtual Organizations"

Network Models have blossomed over the last decade. This model is usually applied to a subculture within a larger organization or a smaller organization. The focus for network cultures is on responsiveness and flexibility relative to customers' changing needs. The organization is not fixed-asset intensive, which allows for greater flexibility. Network cultures achieve success through alliances, joint ventures, outsourcing, and partnering. These groups and alliances are formed for specific purposes and rarely outlive specified projects.

Organizations using network cultures are often found establishing new lines of business and applying innovative technology. They specialize in building strategic alliances and using external resources. The important performance metrics for network organizations are cash-flow and long-term success of the venture.

Compensation strategies for network cultures place an emphasis on individual ventures. The desired competencies are wholly dependent on the needs of specific ventures. The compensation strategy supports the current value of the people or teams with the required competencies. Because of the specific competency requirements, market rates are typically paid for specific skills and competencies. Internal equity is practically disregarded. Rewards are given for positive outcomes under the direct control of individuals or teams.

Top management usually receives a high base salary plus a large long-term incentive based on the success of the venture. This large incentive is usually in terms of ownership because many of these ventures are brand new businesses. Professional-level employees usually receive a competitive market rate along with an aggressive incentive plan based on the contribution to the overall success of the project. In network cultures, the employee structure is typically top heavy and lower-level jobs are outsourced. Because the opportunity for substantial long-term gain is high, the primary lure is the "promise" of future wealth.

The preceding four examples represent the multitude of corporate and organizational cultures in existence. The challenge for compensation design professionals is identifying the specific needs of their organizational cultures and building compensation programs to meet those needs. This process must be continual in order to constantly adjust to cultural shifts within the organization.

Some of the most successful methods of linking compensation strategies to corporate cultures involve a blend of traditional elements with the latest "trendy" ideas in compensation. This combination increases the flexibility of the overall compensation strategy by achieving modernity while retaining the substance the traditional methods provide. Another advantage of the blend is the reduction of the need to completely overhaul the compensation regime every time the trends change.

Whether the design of the compensation strategy is completely traditional, completely modern, or somewhere in between, the key to successful design is assessing where the company is now before looking to where the company leaders aspire to be. The recognition of the current and potential forces of change within the culture of a company is paramount to compensation planning. According to Robert J. Greene, "The dynamic nature of organizational environments and cultures—and even of their visions and missions—mandates that rewards strategies remain in flux. An outdated strategy is almost certain to be a poorly fitting strategy." Greene also shared his opinion on culture and compensation strategy: "Culture will be a key determinant of how well the rewards strategy will work, and cultural definition and evaluation should be major considerations when strategies are formulated, evaluated or revised. Effective rewards strategies will be those that are culturally compatible."

The figure below identifies the numerous factors that play a part in establishing a compensation strategy. Understanding the importance of each factor in each organization will ensure that the compensation strategy will be a successful one.

Figure 4-1. *Establishing a Compensation Package that Fits your Company*

Environmental Influences
Competition ** Technology ** Economics
Social/Political Climate ** Natural Resources
Labor/Skills Supply ** Infrastructure

Vision **Mission**

Culture
• Leadership
• Communication Style
• Degree of:
  • Cultural Sensitivity
  • Diversity
  • Formality
  • Innovation
  • Trust

Organizational Objectives and Strategy

Organizational Structure
• Function/ Department Relationships
• Workplace Design
• Employee Role Definition
• Human Capital Requirements

Compensation Strategy
Recruitment/Staffing — Rewards — Development/Evaluation

Organizational Influences
Size/Complexity ** Industry/Business ** Maturity
Geography/Market Coverage ** Resources Available

COMMUNICATING YOUR COMPENSATION PLAN

The most important way to connect the compensation plan to the organizational plan is through well-organized communication. Without communication the compensation plan is not deemed to be a strong part of corporate culture. Strong communication about the compensation plan is required to keep managers and employees focused on the same beliefs about how their compensation relates to the culture of the organization. In addition, if the defined culture is not communicated *and* practiced, people will have differing beliefs about what the culture should be.

Communication should not only be a mechanism to define or change the organizational culture, but should also be an important piece of the culture itself. All organizations have a communication style that is reflective of their culture. Some have an open style, where employees feel free to express thoughts, ideas, and concerns. Others have a closed style where the culture does not allow for self-expression, but rather survives on the status quo.

Once the compensation strategy has been developed to reflect your desired culture, communication is a critically helpful tool to make the strategy effective and successful. Employees will have more trust and feel more comfortable with their compensation package if they have a good understanding of the overall strategy and the company's goals. If not communicated clearly, employees may feel that they are underpaid or are not receiving the same benefits as others in the workforce.

Not only do the components of a company's package need to be communicated but also the mix of those components and how they tie to the compensation philosophy. For example, an employee may feel that her entire compensation program is less competitive after learning that a friend in a similar position makes $10,000 more in base salary than she does. However, the employee does not take into consideration that her employer also offers a profit sharing plan, which can provide another $15,000 of pay.

Employees need to know the specifics of the overall compensation strategy, and they need to hear it more than once. One of the biggest mistakes Human Resources departments can make is to only communicate a new program or a change once, and then move on to the next program. Take time to follow-up with employees to ensure that they fully understand the programs included in the strategy. Follow-up can include conducting an employee perception survey or creating focus groups to gather feedback about the effectiveness of communication. Having a single point of contact for employees to use as a resource for compensation issues is an exceptional way to gather feedback information, as well as control consistency in message delivery.

Incentive plans, in particular, require a great deal of communication. Because the intent of incentive plans is to motivate employees to achieve corporate goals, employees *must* understand what is required of them. Unfortunately, when companies fail to communicate the desired behaviors and the rewards system, employees often fail to behave in the desired manner.

BEST PRACTICE

The following example from Thomas Flannery, David Hofrichter, and Paul Platten illustrates how desired cultural changes led to compensation strategy readjustment, which led to new messages being communicated to employees.

The management of a company sought to shift their culture from a traditional functional culture to a process-driven culture. The new culture demanded teamwork, a focus on growth, and shared accountability for improving operations. The new values, competencies, and desired behaviors clashed with the company's current compensation program, which primarily rewarded individual performance.

To eliminate the conflict, the company designed a new plan tying salary increases to the growth of team skills. An annual incentive plan was developed based on operating results. Employees were given the option of taking a cash payout or an award of company stock. Lastly, a long-term incentive award of restricted stock emphasized goals of beating the competition.

The resulting message to employees was:

• Teamwork will increase effectiveness.

• Beat the competition in earnings and returns to generate cash for growth.

• View innovation as a long-term enterprise where each employee has a stake.

According to the **Watson Wyatt** 2003-04 Communication ROI study, "Communication is no longer a soft function. It drives business perfor- mance and is a key contributor to organizational success." Financially strong companies studied reported lower employee turnorver rates than their peers and significantly higher total return to shareholders and market value.

When employees feel connected to the business and their own total rewards program, they understand how their actions contribute to personal and corporate success. Technology allows companies to com- municate total rewards communication affordably and on a real-time basis, thus facilitating change as well as specific behaviors that aid continuous improvement.

Communication (whether face-to-face, in print, video, or online) can be useful to:

• encourage employees to take advantage of their benefits

• help them understand the value of their total compensation packages

• facilitate support of organizational values and brand enhancement

• clarify the details of individual performance expectations

• instill the message that employees are valued business partners and key contributors to success.

Forward-thinking companies are developing a "My Total Rewards" intranet portal for employees to access 24/7. This type of customized information generates greater employee interest and understanding because it is personal, simple, and user-friendly. This type of website provides a mechanism for feedback that is valuable to program planners, and it bridges managers to their employers by providing information in a transparent and two-way format. Supervisors must capitalize on their opportunities to reinforce the message that their employees are paid competitively and are appreciated. As the Watson Wyatt report findings suggest, the costs associated with providing this level of integrated total rewards communication far outweigh the costs of miscommunication.

WHAT IT'S WORTH—DETERMINING THE VALUE OF A POSITION OR PERSON TO YOUR COMPANY

A company's culture can characterize how the organization values its employees and the work being done. Cultures will focus on things that motivate and excite the employees to perform collectively rather than just on individual job skills. The compensation strategy, which is aligned directly with the culture, will define how the company formally values positions and the employees who fill those positions.

METRICS

How do organizations determine the value they place on positions or jobs or, more importantly, the work being done? WorldatWork has defined the following traditional methods to placing a value on or evaluating jobs:

- **Simple ranking.** Identify the most important and least important jobs in the job set to create a "job worth hierarchy."

- **Paired-comparison ranking.** Each job is individually compared to every other job. The job of most value from each pairing is noted. A job hierarchy is developed based on the number of times a job is selected.

- **External market pricing.** Job descriptions are used to match survey data. Benchmark jobs are arranged into a hierarchy. Jobs with no market data are slotted into the hierarchy.

- **Classification.** Compares jobs on a whole-job basis. Predefined class descriptions are established for a series of job grades. A job is placed in the classification which best describes it.

- **Job component.** A statistical job evaluation method that uses multiple factor regression analysis. Identifies specific factors and factor weights that help to explain the market pay levels of benchmark jobs. Once the statistical model has been developed, non-benchmark jobs can then be evaluated using the model.

- **Point factor.** Uses defined factors and degrees to establish job value. Job descriptions are compared to the definitions of degrees in order to determine the most appropriate level. The corresponding points for that level are then awarded to the job and combined for all factors to derive a total score.

These methods are frequently used in various combinations.

Like any model, the traditional methods of job evaluation have areas where they excel and areas of weakness.

Pros:

- A formal evaluation method gives meaning to a job and defines its purpose and the reason for its existence in the organization;
- Shows the relative importance an individual job has over other jobs within the organization;
- Best way to compare dissimilar jobs;
- Promotes internal equity and consistency between positions;
- Helps organizations establish the skills and qualifications they need in their positions and what they are willing to pay.

Cons:

- Formal job evaluation methods are not flexible to meet the realities of a constantly changing economy;
- Methods are too narrowly focused and do not allow enough differentiation between evaluating different job families;
- May not reflect external market conditions—depending on the method used;
- By focusing on internal equity, the importance of a competitive pay structure may be ignored;
- Creating a hierarchy of jobs may prevent managers from offering pay for individual needs and situations.

The concept of work evaluation was introduced by Robert L. Heneman of Ohio State University. His assertion is that work evaluation allows organizations to utilize the strengths and weaknesses of traditional job evaluation models within the expanding environment of continuous change. Because of the shifting emphasis to variable pay, companies are seeking simpler methods of work evaluation. However, the simplification of work evaluation still affects variable pay because variable pay rates are often linked to base pay.

Heneman's research examined the current trends in valuing positions. The research indicated that organizations were moving from an emphasis on work evaluation to an emphasis on the external market value. However, there is a concern about the accuracy of the data available from the external market and how it is extracted and analyzed.

Heneman also highlighted legal issues that concern position valuation. Concerns center on the ability to defend pay scales. Without a well-defined work evaluation model, employers are open to challenges by employees due to the interrelationship of incentive pay and benefits with the base salary. Organizations must also be prepared to defend compensation decisions if the Office of Federal Contract Compliance Program examines compensation strategies for equity between genders and ethnic groups. These defenses are much easier if the work evaluation system is well documented.

BEST PRACTICE

Job evaluation

Company name:	Online Apparel Inc.
Problem faced by company:	Online Apparel Inc. was a young online retail company experiencing tremendous growth. New positions were being created daily causing many problems for internal equity between positions. As a result, employees in similar positions were not compensated appropriately.
Compensation solutions:	Competitive base-salary and annual incentive levels were determined for each position. A formal salary structure with grades and ranges was developed based on competitive data. Each job was evaluated using both the simple ranking and external market pricing job evaluation methods. The positions were then assigned to a salary grade within the structure.
Benefit to company:	The company defined the process of creating and evaluating positions. Internal equity was apparent for all positions and across departments. The result was a "job worth" hierarchy from which the company could build upon.

How do organizations place a value on or evaluate the people who accomplish the work? Managers are constantly looking for ways to better communicate how an employee's contribution is perceived by the organization and how it can be improved. The performance of an organization is not only the profit realized but also the investment that is made into the business. Therefore, an employee's performance is not just the work output but also includes the "organizational impact" (positive or negative). The ability to draw ideas out of others, to organize diverse ideas into a cohesive plan, or inspire coworkers would be a positive organizational impact. Negative impacts include a negative outlook, withholding information, or causing unproductive conflict.

Well-structured communication is important to guide employees in the expansion of beliefs about pay-for-performance systems. Many employees believe that these systems only take work output into account. Good communication from management can encourage employees to include organizational impact in the awareness of the structure of compensation systems. Hopefully, this will lead employees to ask:

"How can I increase work output?"
"How can I have a positive impact on the organization?"

Organizations can communicate how they value employees by ensuring that managers communicate more feedback about the employee's performance, job responsibilities, career development, and other decisions that affect them.

Managers need to be emphasizing the "process" of an employee's evaluation, not on the formalities of a form or the standard timing. Providing employees with feedback more frequently will spur more opportunities for employees to discuss problems or other issues they might not discuss during formal "pay increase" related evaluation time. More frequent evaluations will also focus the discussions to look forward to what the employee can accomplish rather than a look back on the past year.

The compensation strategy and corporate culture go hand-in-hand. An effective compensation strategy without defined goals and objectives directly related to the organization's culture is useless. Likewise, an effective corporate culture is unlikely if your compensation strategy is not defined and communicated appropriately to motivate the right behaviors that reflect that culture.

CHAPTER FIVE

ATTRACT AND RETAIN STAR PERFORMERS

OBJECTIVE

To continue the discussion of the importance of compensation to the success of a company, our focus moves from the overall culture to individual workers. The workers who are the lifeblood of any organization are its star performers. They generate the most new ideas and the most new business. The success of any company depends on its ability to attract and retain these star performers.

KEY POINTS

◊ Companies are always looking for new and better ways to attract and retain star performers.

◊ Most companies are now seeking new strategies for using long-term incentives to retain top talent.

◊ Job satisfaction has become the most important piece in attraction and retention.

◊ Individually customizable compensation plans are becoming the primary method to attract and retain top talent.

Attracting and retaining star performers has become more difficult in today's economic environment. Despite negative economic indicators over the past several years, such as fewer IPOs, reports of companies cutting back, loss of stock value, and layoffs, the unemployment rate has been mostly unaffected. This rate is only just now creeping toward 6 percent, which in relative history is still low.

Despite the overall market decline, certain companies have still retained much of their market capitalizations. The companies that maintained their valuations had one thing in common—the quality of their labor forces. The premium in market value is the human capital premium, somthing that is not captured on the balance sheet. The human capital premium is largely a function of star performers.

Consequently, companies are increasingly looking for ways to attract and retain star performers. Since company performance has come under increased scrutiny from stockholders, star performers can help ensure that the company is profitable and well positioned when the economy begins to surge forward.

The best companies encourage all employees to be star performers. This improves the performance of the company and reinforces the view of employees as the most critical assets of the company.

UNDERSTANDING STAR PERFORMER NEEDS

Recent studies indicate job satisfaction has become the most important piece in attraction and retention. In a 2000 New York Times poll, 72 percent of those surveyed chose a lower-paying position with high personal satisfaction over a high-paying job with little personal satisfaction. This emerging trend causes employers to look at compensation differently.

While compensation is a critical component to attract and retain star performers, recent data indicates prospective employees look at factors beyond the size of the paycheck. WorldatWork's 2000 Rewards Study, shown below, identifies several important categories that employees value. Employers need to adjust compensation plans and corporate work environment to better meet the needs of their employees.

Figure 5-1. Overall Results—Importance

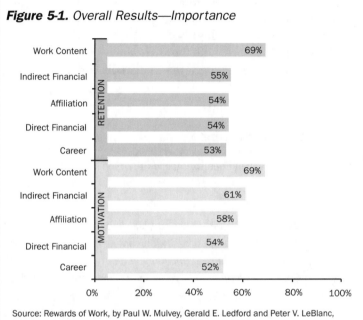

Source: Rewards of Work, by Paul W. Mulvey, Gerald E. Ledford and Peter V. LeBlanc, WorldatWork Journal, Volume 9 Number 3, Third Quarter 2000.

Figure 5-2. Overall—Satisfaction

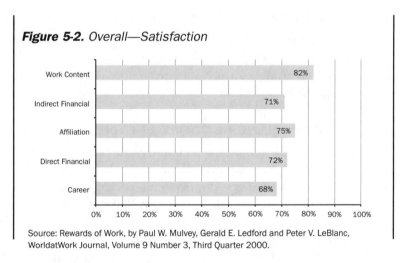

Source: Rewards of Work, by Paul W. Mulvey, Gerald E. Ledford and Peter V. LeBlanc, WorldatWork Journal, Volume 9 Number 3, Third Quarter 2000.

WORK CONTENT

Work content is highly valued by employees. Most individuals want to do something meaningful by working for companies that have a mission or vision that fulfills a purpose larger than profit. Employees also prefer a variety of work to avoid boredom and stagnation. For the same reasons, many individuals like for their work to be challenging. Autonomy is also highly prized by those who want to be treated like an adult at work, with the attendant responsibilities. Employees also want to give feedback that is actually put into use.

BEST PRACTICE

Southwest Airlines exemplifies the type of attitude and culture that meets the work content needs of star performers in its mission statement:

"We are committed to provide our employees a stable work environment with equal opportunity for learning and personal growth. Creativity and innovation are encouraged for improving the effectiveness of Southwest Airlines. Above all, employees will be provided the same concern, respect and caring attitude within the organization that they are expected to share externally with every Southwest customer."

INDIRECT FINANCIAL COMPENSATION

Indirect financial compensation such as benefits and perquisites are also valued by employees. Extra paid vacation days and noncash recognition (public or private) are another commonly used forms of indirect compensation.

DIRECT FINANCIAL COMPENSATION

Direct financial compensation is the typical basis for any compensation package. A market competitive base salary is the nearly mandatory component of any compensation package. Incentives that are linked to various corporate or individual goals are also popular, while ownership in the form of stock grants and options have also been used heavily over the last decade. Other forms of direct financial compensation include cash recognition and premium pay. The next section focuses on specific compensation components utilized to attract and retain star performers.

CAREER

Career progression is also very important to employees. In order to stay motivated about the work that is being done, employees like to believe that their career paths are headed to even more fulfilling positions. Most career issues relate to security and growth. All employees are interested in both groups, but the weighting varies from person to person. People that are focused on security want to be employed and want career consistency. Those focused more on growth want to have advancement opportunities, advanced training, and personal growth experiences.

TRADITIONAL COMPENSATION TO ATTRACT AND RETAIN STAR PERFORMERS

BASE SALARY

In order to properly use base salary as an important piece of the compensation structure, market rates must be established. Pay rates for average employees must be consistent with corporate compensation policy (*i.e.*, 50th percentile, 75th percentile). Star performers with a proven track record typically command base salaries from 75th to 90th percentiles.

ANNUAL INCENTIVES

While competitive base salaries are an integral compensation component, star performers place the greatest emphasis on pay-for-performance programs. Annual incentives, which are typically performance based, are a significant element of the compensation package because they provide the star performers a method to measure themselves. Star performers want the compensation to be linked to their performance because they believe heavily in their own ability to perform and thrive on the tangible recognition of high achievement on the job. Some common annual incentives include:

- **Spot bonuses**—effectively reinforce desired behaviors by immediately recognizing the employee through a non-recurring cash payment.
- **Periodic bonuses**—bonuses that are typically disbursed annually, semiannually, or quarterly based upon established performance

metrics, such as revenue targets, earnings targets, or even nonfinancial measures such as customer satisfaction, attendance policies, etc.

■ **Discretionary awards**—ensure rewards for the true star performance in spite of outside economic factors, such as poor business, industry, or economy performance. These awards should accrue at 1 to 5 percent of payroll and be awarded outside the normal bonus pool.

BEST PRACTICE

Spot bonuses for star employees

Company name:

The Widget Company

Problem faced by company:

The Widget Company began experiencing high turnover among the ranks of its star performers. The company's major concern was how to keep key employees from leaving the company and seeking employment with competitors. In addition, the company was motivated by the knowledge that the cost of replacing talent is even more than the cost of retaining talent.

Compensation solutions:

In any environment where the loss of key people is disrupting the normal flow of business, companies can address the problem through various cash and non-cash retention programs.

The first step in the process is to identify the star employees. In order for retention programs to be an effective use of corporate assets, care should be taken to ensure that the participants are truly the top talent employees that consistently excel.

Spot bonuses were awarded to star performers, which enabled the company to recognize specific employee efforts without a permanent incentive program expense.

Benefit to company:

By implementing a spot bonus program, the Widget Company was able to retain its star employees and motivate other employees to perform on "star" levels.

LONG-TERM INCENTIVES

Long-term incentives are also an important part of compensation for star performers. Long-term incentive plans have historically been the premiere tool for retaining top talent. The heavy usage of stock options as a compensation tool in the 1990s has led to two trends:

- The prevalence of long-term incentives has undergone tremendous growth in the last decade.

> *"We can look back at 1990 and estimate roughly a million option holders and look at the present day and estimate roughly 7 to 10 million option holders ..."*
> —National Center for Employee Ownership

- Equity compensation has become engrained in the culture of many high-tech and start-up companies as a method of attracting top talent due to the reliance on stock options.

However, the current legislative and economic situation is revolutionizing the use of long-term incentive programs. Specifically, after the bursting of the technology bubble, many stock options became worthless. The resultant loss of value made them useless as a retention tool. Along with the older options being underwater, or of no value, new option awards require higher quantities to be given to maintain commensurate value. This leads to overhang issues (the perception of too many shares awarded and reserved for employees as a percentage of total shares outstanding). Additionally, FASB's decision to require the expensing of stock options makes stock option use problematic. Most companies are now developing new strategies for using long-term incentives to retain top talent.

BEST PRACTICES TO ATTRACT AND RETAIN STAR PERFORMERS

As the competitiveness in attracting top talent increases, certain best practices have surfaced. These practices include:

- Employment agreements
- Signing bonuses
- Wealth accumulation through restricted stock awards
- Phantom stock plans
- Nonqualified deferred compensation plans, and
- Other innovations directed at enhancing the employee's quality of life.

EMPLOYMENT AGREEMENTS

Employment agreements are becoming more common in today's tool kit. A survey by William Mercer indicates that the prevalence in employment contracts for top five executives increased by 25 percent from 1998 to 2001. Further increase in the prevalence of employment contracts is expected as result of the economic and political uncertainties in the post 9/11 world (Tauber).

Employment agreements are designed to protect both the employee and the employer. These contracts are designed to make joining a company financially attractive while discouraging the employee from leaving by using financial penalties and disincentives. Key provisions of attractive and retentive employment contracts include:

- Multi-year terms of employment, usually three - five years
- Definition of roles and responsibilities
- Definition of base salary, targeted bonus, and equity compensation
- Change in control protection
- Severance protection in the event the company terminates the employee "not for cause" or the employee terminates for "good reason"
- Noncompete and nonsolicitation clauses that preclude the employee from working for competitors for a one- to two-year period, taking valuable work product/clients/relationships, and/or taking other employees.

SIGN-ON BONUSES

Signing bonuses are also experiencing increased usage. As indicated by the William Mercer study, they rose in prevalence from 20 percent to over 35 percent from 1998 to 2001. Signing bonuses may take many forms but all have the basic promise of financial reward for taking a particular job.

Cash sign-on awards have been historically important in this role and remain so. Both public and private companies commonly use them. Because of the immediacy of the financial gain, employees are partial to this type of signing bonus. However, companies should be aware of Internal Revenue Code §162m, where awards greater than one million dollars are required to have performance criteria if the company expects to take a tax deduction for cash signing bonuses.

In the past, signing bonuses were sometimes delivered in the form of cash loans to the employee. These loans were often forgiven on a time or performance basis. Although private companies still use this practice, the Sarbanes-Oxley Act of 2002 has forbidden its usage among public corporations.

Another common signing bonus tactic: the award of an extremely large stock option grant. The promise of a very large potential gain once carried much allure. This type of bonus has lost its luster due to changes in accounting rules concerning stock options. Shareholder sentiment and stock overhang issues have also reduced the effectiveness of this type of bonus.

Restricted stock has emerged as one of the most useful signing bonus tools. The promise of eventual wealth is often nearly irresistible. The use of restricted stock will be explained shortly along with other wealth accumulation/retention practices.

Long-term incentive awards

Long-term incentives are the best way to attract and especially retain top talent. The attractiveness of long-term incentives for employees is the implicit promise of wealth accumulation if time and/or performance requirements are met. Until recently, the most common form of long-term incentives has been stock options. Options provided a very inexpensive way to attract, retain, and reward employees. However, new accounting requirements, shareholder opinion, and high overhang levels have made stock options both less desirable and less practical. As a result, the following long-term incentives are rising as best practices to attract, retain, and motivate star performers:

1. Restricted stock,
2. Performance share/unit plans, and
3. Nonqualified deferred compensation.

Restricted Stock

Restricted stock is emerging as the "favorite" among long-term incentives for attracting and retaining key talent in publicly traded companies. As such, restricted stock will be described in greater depth than the other forms of long-term incentives.

Definition

A restricted stock award is a grant of stock by an employer to an employee in which the employee's rights to the stock are subject to some type of restriction and risk of forfeiture. Restrictions most often include an employment or length-of-service restriction, also known as time-lapse restricted stock (*i.e.*, vesting over a three- to five-year period). Typically, the employee may not pledge, sell, or transfer the shares of stock until the restrictions lapse; however, the employee receives dividends and voting rights during the restriction period. Once the stated restrictions lapse, the employee obtains full ownership of the unrestricted shares that may be pledged, sold, or transferred. However, in the event the employee does not meet the stated restrictions, the shares are forfeited.

The following are reasons why public companies are increasingly turning to restricted stock awards:

To retain and attract. Restricted stock is a powerful retention tool if the stock award is of significant value—which may not necessarily translate into a significant number of shares. An employee who holds restricted stock can immediately feel the value of the award given the lapse of restrictions. Additionally, in the event an employee terminates and forfeits his or her shares, these shares are then available to use as an attraction tool.

To provide dividend payments to employee stockholders. As opposed to other prevalent equity awards such as stock options, restricted stock allows the recipient to receive dividend payments on the shares awarded. Because of this provision, many companies that return shareholder value via dividends such as utilities or real estate investment trusts—have historically utilized restricted stock awards to reward employees along with the shareholders.

To increase stock ownership. Empirical studies indicate that the most effective way to link shareholder interests with that of executives is through direct equity ownership on behalf of the executive. Restricted stock provides this alignment through ownership accumulation often defined by ownership targets.

To support performance goals. The ultimate goal of all companies is to maximize shareholder value, defined by stock price plus dividends. While restricted stock motivates employees to maximize shareholder value through increasing stock price and dividends, additional performance accelerators may be utilized to achieve critical short-term and/or long-term performance goals that may or may not be immediately recognized by the stock market, such as customer service, business unit profitability, decreasing expenses, etc. For example, vesting periods may be accelerated in the event certain performance goals are achieved, which will provide increased motivation and reinforcement of the goals.

To diversify long-term incentive awards. Restricted stock awards are often utilized in tandem with other long-term incentive vehicles to diversify against a volatile market. In the event a company's stock price declines for external reasons other than the performance of the company, restricted stock allows for employees to retain value, while appreciation-only vehicles, such as stock options, lose their retentive capabilities.

To supplement other pay practices. Because restricted stock has an element of retention and the charge to earnings is spread over a period of time, restricted stock is also utilized to supplement other pay practices such as cash sign-on bonuses, supplemental executive retirement plans, or annual incentives.

Key provisions, accounting impact, tax impact, advantages, and disadvantages are as follows.

Figure 5-3. Restricted Stock

Key Provisions

- Outright grant of shares to executives with restrictions as to sale, transfer and pledging
- Restrictions lapse over a period of time (e.g., three to five years)
- As restrictions lapse, executive has unrestricted shares which he or she may sell, transfer or pledge
- If executive terminates employment, all unvested shares are forfeited
- During restriction period, executive receives dividends and can vote the shares

Earning Impact

- Fair market value at grant charged to earnings over restriction period
- Subsequent appreciation not charged to earnings
- Immediate dilution of EPS for total shares granted

Tax Impact on Executive[1]

- At grant—no tax
- As restrictions lapse–the current market value of vested shares taxed as ordinary income
- Dividends received during restriction period taxed as long-term cap. Gains (15%)

Tax Impact on Company[1]

- At grant—no tax deduction
- As restrictions lapse— company receives tax deduction equal to executive's ordinary income
- At sale—no tax deduction
- Dividends paid during restriction period are not deductible

[1] *Assumes 83(b) election is not made. If an 83(b) is made, executive recognizes income on the date the restricted stock was issued, and the company receives an immediate tax deduction for the initial value of the shares (but not for subsequent appreciation during the restriction period); dividends paid during the restriction period are not deductible.*

Advantages

- No executive investment required
- Promotes immediate stock ownership
- Charge to earnings is fixed at time of grant
- If stock appreciates, company's tax deduction exceeds fixed charge to earnings
- Aligns executive's interests with shareholders
- Recognizable to most executives
- Offers executive potentially long-term appreciation as company grows

Disadvantages

- Immediate dilution of EPS
- Executive may incur tax liability before shares are sold
- Executive may pay tax (at vesting) at a higher stock price than the date of sale

Figure 5-4. *Restricted Stock works as follows ...*

Timing	Years	
	1	5
Restricted Stock	Grant	Restriction Lapse
Fair Market Value:	$5	$10
Dividends:	$0	$1.00
Executive Investment:	$0	$0
Executive Gain:	$0	$11.00 (Ordinary Income)
Executive Tax [1]:	$0	$3.65 Tax Due
	($10.00 X 35%) + ($1.00 X 15%)	
Executive Net Gain: (After Tax)	$0	$7.35 Net Gain

(1) Assumes the executive is subject to an ordinary income tax rate of 35%. If an 83(b) election was made within 30 days of the award, the executive would be taxed on the fair value of the stock at grant as ordinary income, with subsequent appreciation treated as a capital gain. Dividend is taxed at long-term capital gains rate. 83(b) elections are not typically with a high prices stock because the executive cannot recover taxes paid at grant if he or she forfeits the shares or if the shares decrease in value.

Figure 5-5. *Performance Units*

Key Provisions

- Grants of units with absolute dollar value (e.g., $30) with payout contingent on meeting stated performance targets over a specified period (usually three to five years)
- To the extent targets are met, the dollar value of units is payable in cash and/ or stock
- If minimum performance threshold is not met, units are forfeited
- Frequently used as financing mechanism for equity plans

Tax Impact on Executive[1]

- At grant—no tax
- At payment – payout taxed as ordinary income

Tax Impact on Company[1]

- At grant—no tax deduction
- At payment—company receives tax deduction equal to executive's ordinary income

Earnings Impact

- Value of performance units is charged to earnings to the degree goals are achieved over the performance period
- Charge to Earnings is fixed assuming maximum payout; any payout less than maximum is reconciled at the end of the performance period

Advantages

- Fixed Charge to Earnings
- No executive investment required
- Company receives tax deduction
- Performance oriented for non market activity / strategic initiatives
- Potential maximum charge to earnings is fixed at grant
- Executive's tax liability can be paid out of award
- Helps finance options
- No dilution of shares outstanding unless paid in stock

Disadvantages

- Difficulty in setting performance targets, especially in cyclical business
- Does not lead to direct stock ownership unless paid in stock
- May result in substantial cash outflows if paid in cash
- No tax advantages to executive

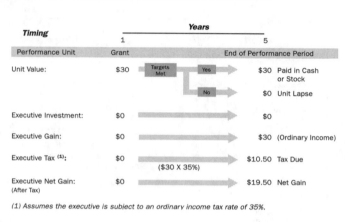

Figure 5-6. *Performance Units work as follows ...*

(1) Assumes the executive is subject to an ordinary income tax rate of 35%.

Performance Share/Unit Plans

A performance share plan is a stock (or stock unit award plan) where the payout is contingent upon achievement of certain predetermined external or internal goals during a specified period (typically three to five years) before the recipient has the right to the stock. The employee receiving the shares pays ordinary income tax. A performance unit plan (PUP) is similar to a performance share plan, except the unit value is not related to stock. Both plans are typically best used when tied to long-term strategic objectives. Key provisions for both types of plans follow:

Table 5-1. *Tax/Earnings Impact — Performance Shares*

Tax	▪ Executive - ordinary income tax at payout ▪ Employer - matching tax deduction at payout
Earnings	▪ Stock-settled - fair value fixed at grant and recognized over service (vesting) period ▪ Cash-settled – variable charge to earnings over service (vesting) period

Table 5-2. *Example — Performance Shares*

	If average return on equity is	Percent performance shares earned is	Number of shares earned
	18% or more	150%	1,500
	17%	130%	1,300
	16%	115%	1,150
Target	15%	100%	1,000
	14%	90%	900
	13%	80%	800
	12%	70%	700
	Less than 12%	0%	0

Nonqualified deferred compensation

Nonqualified deferred compensation historically has been a solid way for companies to allow top employees to accumulate wealth while retaining the employee. However, with the demise of stock option use, nonqualified deferred compensation is resurging as a key vehicle to attract and retain top talent via significant wealth building opportunity.

DEFINITION

A nonqualified plan is an employer-sponsored retirement plan that does not meet the qualified plan requirements (and is therefore not subject to their limitations) under Internal Revenue Code §401. Further, it is generally an unfunded plan maintained primarily to provide deferred compensation for a select group of management or highly compensated employees (ERISA, §201(2)).

Private and public companies are offering nonqualified plans for the following reasons:

- To attract and retain key employees (most major employers offer some form of nonqualified plan).
- To provide additional tax deferral and financial planning opportunities for key employees.
- To assist midcareer executives in the accumulation of retirement assets (in 2003, many individuals have qualified plan balances that have shrunk in value over the past several years. Nonqualified plans offer customizable methods for participants to set aside additional funds).
- To provide key employees at higher levels of compensation with a retirement vehicle that takes into account their entire compensation.
- To make up for qualified plan contribution limitations: in 2004, qualified plans limited employees to the lesser of $13,000 in pre-tax contributions (deferrals), or 100 percent of compensation; or, $41,000 in total annual additions and benefits limited to first $205,000 of compensation.
- To make up for lost benefits: discrimination testing can reduce contributions and benefits of qualified plans for highly compensated employees.
- To enable, in certain circumstances, the deferral of gains from equity compensation plans that are near realization.

By their nature, nonqualified plans are very flexible in design. This makes them easy to tailor to accomplish corporate objectives. Certain requirements that must be followed are as follows:

- The plan design must avoid "constructive receipt."
- The plan must be "unfunded" for ERISA and IRC purposes and apply to a "select group of management" (*a.k.a* the "Top Hat" group). The benefits offered are an obligation of the company.
- Plans may offer notional deferral opportunities integrated with qualified plan offering (so-called "Mirror" plans), or may offer completely different alternatives (fixed rate options are increasingly popular), or may take the form of defined benefit plans.
- Emergency and early withdrawals from the plan are possible—but are generally subject to penalties.
- Deferral and distribution elections must be made prior to the service period to which compensation relates.
- Distributions cannot be rolled over to IRA or tax qualified plans.

The following is a summary of various nonqualified plans:

Table 5-A

Salary and Bonus Deferral	Provides executives the opportunity to defer bonus and base salary into the future (tax deferral) and receive tax deferred earnings build-up within the plan. Participants are allowed to defer all or portion of salary and annual bonus. Deferred amounts are invested in one or more investment vehicles. Often used in conjunction with DC SERP. Use of Rabbi Trust is typical.
Salary and Bonus Deferrals with Company Match or Contribution	Similar to salary and bonus deferral except the company matches a portion of the participant's deferrals or makes contributions often based on company performance. The company's match or contributions are sometimes converted into common stock equivalents. Gives company a way to link company performance and share ownership to executive retirement savings. Vesting schedules typically apply for employer match and contributions. Often used as an alternative to a defined contribution SERP. Use of Rabbi Trust is typical.
Defined Contribution SERP	Provides a mechanism to restore benefits to "highly compensated" employees lost due to limitations on qualified plans annual employee deferral limits. Pre-determined employee and employer contributions are invested in one or more investment vehicles, often including company stock. Employer contributions typically make up benefits lost in the 401k plan or provide additional contributions for key executives. Use of a Rabbi Trust to segregate assets is typical. Corporate owned life insurance or mutual funds may be used in conjunction with Rabbi Trust to "fund" benefits.
Defined Benefit SERP	Intended to restore benefits lost from qualified plans or provide additional retirement benefits to senior executives who often join the company at mid career. Supplemental retirement benefit expressed as a percentage of final salary or a flat amount. Similar to qualified pension plans with participation restricted to a "select group of management". A supplemental death benefit is often included. Corporate owned life insurance may be used in conjunction with Rabbi Trust to "fund" benefits.
Comprehensive Executive Benefit Plan	A comprehensive program that may include death, disability, and retirement benefits. Typically funded through some sort of insurance program.

Figure 5-7. Deferred Compensation Plans

Key Provisions	Tax Impact on Executive	Advantages
■ An arrangement whereby executive is credited with contributions to a deferred compensation account.	■ At grant—no tax ■ At payout-ordinary Income	■ Discretionary, discriminatory contributions. ■ Does not dilute actual ownership. ■ Easy to understand ■ Can be very retentive
■ Executive may elect to defer income on pre-tax basis.	**Tax Impact on Company** ■ At grant— 　■ cash-no tax deduction. 　■ P& L –deferred tax asset. ■ At payment—company receives tax deduction equal to executive's ordinary income	**Disadvantages** ■ Unpredictable charge to earnings if liability is not hedged with an asset ■ Does not lead to direct stock ownership. ■ Participants are unsecured creditors of the company.
■ Account balances are credited with investment earnings 　■ Company may declare a rate, or allow executive to control asset allocation from several investment options ■ Payable in cash	**Earnings Impact** ■ Employer contributions accrued over vesting period. ■ Appreciation is charged to earnings as credited to account balance	

INNOVATIVE COMPENSATION PACKAGES: WHEN MONEY IS NOT ENOUGH

Unfortunately for human resource professionals, attraction, retention, and motivation of top talent is not always strictly related to financial gain. People may leave well-paid jobs for personal reasons that are not linked to finances. Compensation developers must be aware of other issues that motivate top performers.

Common reasons people leave jobs include:

- Lack of opportunity
- Desire to balance work/family hours
- Uncertainty in the workplace
- Disagreement with supervisors
- View of short tenure (free agent attitude)
- Relocation
- Work hours
- Retirement
- Return to school

BEST PRACTICES TO ATTRACT AND RETAIN TOP TALENT, WHEN MONEY IS NOT ENOUGH

When people fail to respond solely to financial remuneration, compensation package design gets much more interesting. Several best practices in this situation are described here:

- Planners actually enlist the employee's assistance to design a plan that is intended to keep them at the company. The development of a personal retention plan involves the identification of the things that are most important to the employee during the hiring process. A personalized plan is then designed around the needs of the employee and the employer.
- Internal escape hatches work well to prevent talent leakage. Companies with this type of program allow employees to apply for other positions within the company. Internal mobility allows the employee to bypass poor supervisory relationships and career mobility issues while the company retains the employee and reduces the potential loss of a human capital investment.
- Flexible hours assist employees seeking work-life balance. A Bureau of Labor Statistics study on the American workforce indicates the number of hours worked per married couple has increased 14 hours per week over the last 30 years.

Companies have attempted to help employees to achieve balance by:

- Compressing the work week to four days
- Offering telecommuting from home
- Allowing work hour shift to reduce commute times

As business has become more stressful, employees are seeking time to recenter and refocus. Fortunately, companies are beginning to develop ways to help their employees do just that. The use of sabbaticals is becoming more common. The length and purpose may differ for each company and individual, but the increased availability of sabbaticals is an indication that companies recognize that even top performers may need some time away.

Dependent care programs have also become important. Companies are acknowledging that people perform better when their dependents are well cared for. Dependent care gained importance with the massive increase of two-career families. Demographic changes have made "dependent" as likely to be used for the elderly as for children.

Other changes in the working environment include the reduction of rigidity in corporate spaces. Business casual attire is more prevalent. Workspaces are more friendly and inviting, with more care taken on aesthetics. Companies are trying to become more open and friendly to promote positive feelings toward the work environment.

Table 5-B

NAIC's Low Cost Retention Programs			
Program	Percentage of Employees Using the Program	Ability to Retain Employees	Cost
Four-day workweek/flex-time	85%	High	Low
Business-casual dress code with Friday as jeans day	99%	High	Low
Infants in the workplace	2%	High	Low
Emergency financial assistance	4%	Moderate	Low
No-interest computer loans	20%	Moderate	Moderate
Telecommuting	5%	High	Moderate

Source: "Low-cost Programs to Keep Employees Hooked", by Brent Rober, Workspan 11/2002.

In the event the employee terminates, the best companies keep an alumni list from which to recruit in the future. This will become increasingly important with predictions of labor shortages in the coming decade. Recruiting employees who have previous experience with the company can be quite lucrative, because both entities have some prior knowledge of the other.

WHAT DOES THE FUTURE HOLD?

Attracting and retaining star performers has and will continue to be one of the most critical components for companies to outperform their peers. While there has been focus on financial and nonfinancial best practices to attract and retain star performers, it is clear there is an emerging trend to tailor the total rewards packages to the ever-diversifying needs of employees. These tailored total rewards packages provide a typical base salary with a variety of choices for employees. Employees are allowed to customize the individual compensation plans from a set dollar amount of targeted annual incentive dollars, targeted long-term incentive dollars, time off, perquisites, increased health-care coverage, long-term disability coverage, and/or dependent care coverage.

This type of compensation strategy will allow companies to maximize the utility provided to employees for each compensation dollar spent, while recognizing that each employee has different needs. The customizable aspect of this type of plan will allow the flexibility to cope with the increasingly variable needs of the rapidly diversifying workforce. Social, demographic, economic, and political trends suggest that individually customizable compensation plans will become the primary method to attract and retain top talent.

CHAPTER SIX

REWARDING EMPLOYEES AND MANAGING THE BOTTOM LINE

OBJECTIVE

So far, the discussion about total rewards has focused on attracting, retaining, and motivating talent. Corporate culture has also been discussed because culture affects the design of the compensation program and culture is affected by the types of employees hired by the organization.

KEY POINTS

◊ Use variable incentives to reduce fixed costs.
◊ Properly designed programs can have significant impact on employee behavior.
◊ Increased use of pay-for-performance increases opportunities for significant rewards for employees.
◊ Human resource professionals can have significant impact through compensation programs.

Every compensation program must answer the following questions:
- How does the organization attract, retain, and motivate top talent?
- How does the organization reinforce its culture through its compensation policies?
- How are employees rewarded while costs are contained and the bottom line is managed?

The last question leads to a discussion of one of the toughest issues for human resource professionals. Typically, human resources professionals feel like they have little impact on top-line performance and their contributions are difficult to quantify.

In reality, HR professionals have a large influence on labor efficiencies. Typically, through the design of compensation packages, compensation is the largest expense line in most organizations, which makes labor efficiencies even more important.

Hence, HR activities have bottom-line organizational importance.

HOW ARE COMPENSATION AND INCENTIVE PROGRAMS DESIGNED TO MAXIMIZE RESULTS?

Compensation and incentive programs must be directly related to the performance of the company. Achieving a performance-driven program means reducing fixed-cost compensation while increasing or providing more opportunity for employees to receive variable or incentive pay. These opportunities should actually give employees a chance to earn more. The ultimate goal: to achieve a pay-for-performance design where the pay element of compensation is driven by the overall results of the organization.

Pay-for-performance is the most efficient way to design an organizational compensation structure. This type of program allows organizations to most appropriately cope with the reality of human capital. As stated earlier, compensation is usually the largest expense for an organization. However, the human capital represented by that expense is one of the most valuable assets in any organization. This human capital serves as a primary driver for organizational success.

Since employees represent a valuable pool of assets, that happen to be extremely mobile, the challenge for the human resources departments is to attract, retain, and motivate for maximum results.

Results are maximized by managing the bottom line. The easiest way to manage the bottom line is through the retention of current employees. It is important to keep employees satisfied and challenged so they will not think about working elsewhere. The primary importance of retention is how it affects costs. The cost for hiring, retraining, and cultural indoctrination are several multiples of the cost of retention.

The human resources professional must assure that the overall compensation program is appropriately balancing costs and benefits for each reward program. Several different elements form the costs:

- **Implementation.** The startup costs of a program. These costs derive from the cost of the design program and the development of any necessary infrastructure, including communication expenses. Training costs for the program staff may be included in the implementation costs.
- **Rewards.** The actual costs attributed to the reward. This is the cost to the company, not the value to the employee.
- **Administration.** These program maintenance costs include recordkeeping, infrastructure maintenance, and help-desk services attributable to a particular rewards program.

In a cost-benefit analysis, the benefits are defined as those that create value for the organization. Some examples are:

- **Stronger motivation.** Employees are better motivated, which usually leads to better results.
- **Overall morale.** The mood around the organization is good and employees are generally positive about their work.
- **Builds structure and culture.** As said before, a well-designed compensation system can help enhance the culture (which can lead to structure) by influencing the types of employees that are attracted and retained.

BEST PRACTICE

Incentive program that maximizes results

Company name: **XYZ Company**

Problem faced by company:
XYZ Company had a limited management incentive program. All managers received the same payout regardless of performance or job level. Individual or divisional goals were not factored into the payout equation; in fact, no minimum performance goals were required in order to earn an award.

Because the incentive awards were not directly tied to performance, XYZ Company wasted corporate assets paying managers additional compensation without receiving a performance benefit.

Compensation solutions:
During a down market, companies should take care to ensure that compensation programs are tied to measurable goals that support the goals and strategy of the company. By tying incentives to performance, company employees are better motivated and amply rewarded.

The first step in the process is to identify who the incentive plan participants will be.

Once the determination of participants is complete, a comprehensive market analysis should be conducted for the individuals to ensure that their current total direct compensation is competitive, as this forms the basis from which the incentive program will be designed.

The design of the incentive program first and foremost should provide incentive payouts tied to measurable and stated performance goals. Awards should be a combination of corporate, division, and individual goals (that make sense for the particular position), and payouts should not occur unless the participant has met a minimum standard of performance. To assist with the determination of payouts, the company should structure a metric of minimum, target, and maximum performance and pay a comparable incentive for achieving the specific levels.

In addition, incentive payout targets (correspondingly minimums and maximums) should vary based on the job level. The executive group should receive the highest incentive potential and then other participants should be eligible for an award tiered down from the executive level, corresponding to their worth within the company.

Benefit to company:
By implementing a pay-for-performance incentive plan, XYZ Company was able to target its limited payroll budget more effectively and increase production among its employees.

Managing the balance is important, because the programs will be evaluated by people other than the human resources department. The finance department will want to see reductions in overall fixed costs. In the realm of compensation, these fixed costs primarily come from base salaries.

In order to best balance costs and benefits in a method that appeals to management, the structure of the program should be built around the following principles: Base salary should be kept below the going market rate and above-market-rate incentives should be provided and tied to performance.

Employee benefits should also be managed for bottom-line effectiveness. The perceived benefits should be compared to the actual cost of the benefit. For example, younger employees place less value on health benefits than older employees. Therefore, a company with mostly young employees does not receive much value for the dollar of health care provided. As with pay, companies should attempt to reduce the amount of fixed benefits. In order to reduce the amount, fixed-cost benefit programs should be evaluated frequently.

How does this approach to managing compensation and benefit costs affect today's businesses?

COMPENSATING EMPLOYEES IN A SOFTER ECONOMY

The events of recent years have been indicators of the difficult economic climate for the business world. Trust in the stock market has lessened as result of political uncertainty abroad and ethics issues at home. In this environment, companies find themselves asking:

- How can a compensation and reward strategy still attract and retain employees?
- How is change handled when the times get tough?

Specific characteristics of soft economies factor into the design of compensation programs. The impact on the labor market is one of the key characteristics. The labor market operates according to the law of supply and demand, and during soft economic times, the labor market shifts from a seller's market to a buyer's market. Stiff competition for employment increases. More talent is available for companies to choose from.

The impact of this market shift directly influences the bottom line through the structure of compensation packages. In a buyer's market, the negotiating power has come to rest with the companies.

This in turn reduces the pressure on companies to provide financially lucrative compensation packages, because they are choosing from a wider talent pool.

This environment is in comparison to that of the late 1990s, when stock options, signing bonuses, and perquisites were used to bid for the services of members of a tight labor market. The high demand for labor at that point in time led to low unemployment and high labor prices. In today's softer economy, employees are happy with just having a job. They do not need as much incentive. During soft economic times, employees work harder with fewer resources.

METRICS

Compensation and reward programs should be reevaluated during periods of belt tightening. Typically, rewards packages are subject to cutbacks as are other budget items. Base salary is one of the areas most affected by changes in the budget. Layoffs, which have become fairly common, are a somewhat demoralizing method of reducing the base salary budget. Finding an alternative to layoffs is desirable for employee morale purposes.

Salary cuts

Salary cuts can result in bottom line savings. Salary freezes allow a savings for the company by not giving the standard cost-of-living increase. The least painful method of reducing the salary budget is to allow for a slight increase in base pay that does not exactly reach the cost-of-living increase. Benefits are also affected as employers often ask employees to cover more of the costs.

During any budget tightening, a premium is placed on communication. Organizations must give employees the assurance that they are valuable parts to the organization. The financial status of the organization must be explained so employees understand why cutbacks are necessary. Good communication reduces the fear and apprehension of employees. Productivity is reduced when employees are constantly worried about what might happen next.

Low-cost rewards

Difficult economic times provide great opportunities for human resource professionals to display their creativity. Novel low-cost rewards can be used to make employees feel valued, despite the current economic situation. These rewards can be used instead of cash or stock options. Typical solutions are nonmonetary but still provide acknowledgement of a job well done. The important point is to show the employee that he or she is valued at the least possible cost.

Many low-cost methods exist to provide a mental boost for employees. Some of these include:

- An extra paid day off
- More authority to take initiative
- More prominent roles, such as project leader
- A formalized thank you
- An occasional extended lunch break
- Any initiative that makes employees feel special

Performance rewards

Companies reevaluate how much they are paying out during tough times. They also reevaluate the methods with which they reward employees and how they measure the criteria for earning rewards. Companies need to determine:

- What is good performance?
- How is good performance evaluated?
- How are performance evaluation systems evaluated?

During this evaluation, companies need to reconsider how performance is being measured and evaluated to align with company goals. The rewards system should also be evaluated for performance in the current labor market.

Recent economic factors have forced companies to change the mix of elements in the rewards package. One of the types of compensation that has changed in usage over the last several years is the stock option. During the bull market of the late 1990s, stock options were used as a highly desired tool to attract talent. However, options have been underwater for years, which reduces the attraction. Options have now shifted in usage to a retention tool. Now, they are typically used to reward current employees and to align their long-term behaviors with those of the company.

Rewards during bankruptcy

Bankruptcy presents unique challenges to an organization. Special care must be taken to design rewards systems that keep employees focused during restructuring or reorganization. The objective during the bankruptcy period is to maximize creditor repayment. In order to meet that objective, employees must be free of the fear that can occur during uncertain times. Employees also have to be motivated to work until the bitter end. To ensure that employees remain motivated, cash payments and bonuses should be paid as reward for behaviors that maximize creditor repayment. Retention bonuses should also be used to encourage employees to stay with the company despite the possibility of the company going under. Well-designed and generous severance packages can also help convince employees to stay a little longer.

The soft economy does more than affect the labor economics. It also affects the ability of companies to achieve results. In a soft economy, job performance that can directly influence more positive results is more important than ever. Compensation packages can be used to encourage a change in how employees perform.

USING COMPENSATION TO ENCOURAGE PERFORMANCE CHANGES

To shift employee attitudes about performance, high performers must be recognized and rewarded. Ongoing systems must be in place, be efficient, and be significant enough to encourage change.

In order for change to happen, people have to understand and embrace it. They need to be enthusiastic and excited about making good things happen. Human resources can have this impact by motivating employees and encouraging performance through compensation policies.

Human resources can be a catalyst for the turnaround of companies through compensation programs. Properly designed rewards programs can provide huge positive results. As with any compensation issue, design is the key. The rewards program must motivate the right behavior. In order to do that, the designer must start with the big picture. The overall organizational goals must be evaluated—how are these goals to be achieved? Once these goals are understood, the individual and team components should be outlined. After clearly defining individual and group goals and objectives, rewards should be used to encourage the fulfillment of those goals and objectives.

This premium on performance-based compensation is contrary to traditional forms of compensation. In the past, bonuses and other types of compensation were based on seniority. This encouraged retention but did not place any weight on performance. Therefore, a malaise of contentment settled upon companies. Employees came to expect giveaways for what essentially was the ability to wake up and to find the office on most mornings. This atmosphere discouraged risk taking and contributed to the disillusionment of workers with high ideals and standards.

Now, in order for companies to compete, they must receive maximum contributions from the labor force. The business environment is too competitive to waste resources on someone who goes to work each day as cubicle filler. Companies have begun the shift to pay-for-performance. This type of pay encourages measurable initiative, which leads to increased organizational growth.

In order to gain maximum benefit from a pay-for-performance program, the organization must foster a workplace environment that allows opportunity for both intrinsic and extrinsic rewards. These opportunities must be directed in a fashion that guides appropriate result-driven behaviors. Rewards must be:

- Perceived as meaningful and valuable
- Based on objective and attainable goals
- Based on achieving desired performance levels
- Open and available to all and
- Balanced between intrinsic and extrinsic values.

Availability of rewards is important because competitive, exclusionary rewards can only serve as divisive influences in the workplace.

DEFINITION

Intrinsic rewards are those that are more psychological and internal in benefit for the employee. This could be the internal satisfaction of knowing the job or task was done well. This type of reward could also be the recognition of accomplishment by peers or supervisors. Basically, this category of rewards creates good, positive feeling inside the employee.

The external class of rewards is referred to as extrinsic rewards. This group is more material in nature. These types of rewards typically have a fairly substantial monetary value. Included in this grouping are cash, stock, stock options, and warrants. With these types of rewards, employees can purchase the things that make them happy.

As mentioned earlier, each program should be subjected to cost-benefit analysis. This process will allow companies to find the rewards mix that best serves to accomplish their goals. This mix will change as circumstances change.

Again, a key example of how changing times influence the choice of rewards is the usage of stock options in the late 1990s. Options were extremely popular due to the great value for both employers and employees. For employers, they were extremely cheap—especially on the accounting books. Employees viewed them as a way to achieve greater wealth. After years of underwater options and changes in the accounting treatment of options, neither employers nor employees are as interested in stock options as a form of reward.

When evaluating the impact of a shift in rewards systems, human resource professionals should be able to recognize and distinguish between two types of employees:

- The **value maintainer** is interested in keeping the status quo. This group of employees will do what they are asked to do, but they studiously avoid the outward display of anything that even remotely approaches initiative.
- The other group is called **value creators.** This is the creative class that adds new life to the organization. These people are oriented

toward developing and making positive change. An important goal of the rewards programs should be to reward and motivate value creators.

Performance programs can encourage both short- and long-term organizational growth. Many different methods exist to encourage performance through pay. The two primary classes of performance pay are fixed and variable.

Fixed compensation is typically the first method companies explore. On the surface, fixed compensation adjustment is appealing. Types of fixed rewards for performance include merit raises, perquisites, and benefits. However, the savvy human resources professional will quickly realize that these types of performance rewards carry significant long-term impact because the rewards essentially become annuities. Therefore, human resource professionals should use extreme caution when adjusting elements of the rewards package that are perceived as fixed.

A better alternative is the usage of variable compensation. Variable compensation is the element of compensation that is "at risk." It changes year after year depending on performance of the individual, team, or organization. The key to designing a variable compensation package is to identify the strongest correlations between compensation initiatives and overall organizational performance. These correlations affect the efficiency in this type of compensation arrangement. The efficiency is caused primarily by employees participating in and directly benefiting from the organizational results.

USING VARIABLE COMPENSATION

Variable compensation plans must be tied to economic factors that are important for the success of the organization. The keys to designing a variable compensation structure include the answers to:

- What behavior is the organization trying to motivate?
- What behavior is it currently getting?
- What are the actual goals of the company?
- How is achievement of the goals measured?

The last question is very important to the design, because the answer will directly affect the metrics of performance programs.

METRICS

Essentially two types of metrics are used to measure the progress toward the goals. Financial metrics such as cash flows, earnings, and total shareholder return examine the overall organizational performance. Individual or team metrics, including sales and production efficiencies, measure how a particular employee or small group of employees performed to assist in the achievement of organizational goals.

Variable compensation, used properly, has a great potential to positively impact the organization. This type of compensation offers a method for reducing or, at least, not raising fixed costs. Variable compensation also provides upside potential (and motivation) for employees. The primary concern with variable compensation is whether overall results are in line with the metrics in use. When developing reward systems based on variable compensation, the reward opportunities should be significant and competitive with market practices.

HOW DOES PAY RELATE TO PERFORMANCE?

Pay is related to performance through the use of different measurements that are chosen to best define and describe the relationship between the performance of an individual and the overall performance of the company.

METRICS

Performance can be measured many different ways. Typically, the overall suite of measurements is chosen to provide an appropriate balance between several pairings of attributes. Typical attribute pairs are individual/group, short-term/long-term, and qualitative/quantitative.

Almost every performance evaluation/reward system strives to find the appropriate balance between individual and group performance. Individual goals are important because they hold the individual responsible for behavior. Individual goals are balanced with group goals, which assist in the promotion of group or even corporate unity. Typically, the balance between these two types is dependent on the responsibilities and position of the person or group being evaluated. An executive's evaluation would emphasize group performance while a lineworker's evaluation would emphasize his or her own performance.

Another important set of attributes is the time horizon of the evaluation. Short-term is used to describe any measurement within one performance period (usually a year). Long-term is typically three to five years. Like the other sets of metrics, the balance between the two is important and differs depending on the position of the employee. Once again, the starkest contrasts are between the executive level and the lineworkers. Executives are expected have a longer time horizon and more ability to affect long-term plans, so they have more long-term measurements built into their performance evaluations and reward programs.

The technique of measurement is also important. Quantitative measurements are numbers-driven and are typically straightforward. Examples include share price, net income, and revenue. Qualitative measurements are more difficult to comprehend, and they are also difficult to evaluate. Often, companies will try to force qualitative evaluations into a quantitative format. Qualitative measurements may include teamwork, safety, and customer service.

How are rewards paid out?

Typical variable rewards are disbursed in either cash or some type of equity instrument. The actual choice depends on the need of the company. If cash is available and share dilution is a concern, then rewards should be cash. If the company is cash strapped, then equity rewards are more likely.

The structure of rewards depends on the responsibility associated with each given position. For all positions, goals and metrics must be clearly defined. Performance targets must be legitimately attainable. Line-of-sight (an individual's ability to affect the overall organization) is also taken into account. Evaluations should be regular and consistent.

Payouts are different for different levels of employees. These levels are based primarily on the responsibilities and requirements of the position. Also, the format and parameters for measurement are dependent on the level of the employee.

The group that typically receives the largest payout from rewards programs is the executive group. This group participates in both time horizons of rewards more often than other employees.

Two main categories for variable compensation are annual incentives and long-term incentives.

Annual incentives. Annual incentives are the near-term element of variable compensation. Typically, this group of incentives is disbursed in cash as a reward for short-term performance. This is primarily an individual performance measurement at the lower levels in a company. Higher up the corporate ladder, short-term incentives are increasingly based on group or organizational measurements, which are very often quantitative measurements such as net income. Targets for annual incentives must be set early and well communicated so employees have a reasonable opportunity to meet performance goals. Payout for short-term incentives must be timely to reinforce the linkage between the reward and the desired behavior. Payouts for annual incentives are typically expressed as a percentage of the base salary.

Long-term incentives. Long-term incentives are linked to longer-term goals. Rewards can be much larger than for short-term achievements. Long-term incentives are intended to align employees, especially executives, with the interests of stockholders. Optimally, employees will be encouraged to work toward an overall direction. Part of the intention of long-term incentives is to prevent the sacrifice of the long-term good for short-term results. This type of incentives is more frequent among executives, but trends are suggesting that employees at all levels are becoming increasingly involved in long-term incentives.

Many different methods are available for use as long-term incentives. Cash is sometimes used, but typically equity or equity equivalents are used in long-term rewards. One of the best tools to use for this type of reward is restricted stock, because stock options, the primary method of the last few decades, are under media, regulatory, political, and investor scrutiny.

CHAPTER SEVEN

WHEN THE BEST SHOULD EARN THE MOST

OBJECTIVE

Paying for top performance is a compensation philosophy many organizations discuss as a critical component to success. Therefore, it is no coincidence that the highest performing companies adhere to the philosophy: *reward the best, push the rest.*

KEY POINTS

◊ Rewarding great performers is the best way to motivate and retain top talent.
◊ The best employees should be rewarded while the remaining employee population should be pushed to become the best.
◊ *Reward the best, push the rest* should be part of a compensation philosophy that directly links to the goals and objectives of the company by incorporating performance management.

Rewarding "top-performing employees" does not mean rewarding solely high-level employees. Organizations are using performance pay for middle managers, professionals and hourly workers, determined not to let the depressed business climate lead to a depressed workforce.

—Steve Bates

Rewarding great performers is the best way to motivate and retain top talent. These are the people most responsible for the achievement of organizational goals and they should be rewarded in an appropriate fashion. Everyone else should be encouraged to become top performers by the example of the rewards given to the top people.

A Watson Wyatt survey found that companies providing variable pay to their best workers are 68 percent more likely than other firms to report outstanding financial performance (Bates). While this statistic may be a positive correlation in itself, it is likely this statistic is indicative of a management style with a human resource focus that recognizes pay-for-performance as a key component to attract, retain, and motivate outstanding people. The variable pay/outstanding financial performance correlation is also supported by the belief that top talent prefers variable pay as a way to acknowledge high levels of performance.

VARIABLE REWARD ALTERNATIVES

Two-thirds of U.S. companies currently use some sort of variable pay. However, it's being used for fewer employees, but those receiving it are getting more. Historically, in the 1980s and into the 1990s, all employees received a standard salary increase of 8–10 percent and any drop below that level would cause resentment. However, since 2000, the average employee salary increase has dropped to approximately 3–4 percent. Companies are no longer relying on plain vanilla, across the board merit increases. Instead, companies are increasingly relying on performance rewards to provide additional compensation opportunities for star performers, while average and below average performers are receiving a decreasing portion of the profit pie.

METRICS

While pay-for-performance can be measured on various levels such as individual performance, team performance, corporate performance, business unit performance, etc., it can also be delivered through various compensation vehicles, such as base salary increases, annual incentives, and/or long-term incentives.

How companies effectively reward top performance, while retaining the remaining employee population, has historically been a tricky proposition. However, some of the top performing companies in the U.S. have relied upon the following vehicles to reinforce a dramatic pay-for-performance program:

- Additional base salary increases
- Annual incentives
- Long-term incentives.

ADDITIONAL BASE SALARY INCREASES

While most companies have decreased all employee annual salary increases to approximately 3–4 percent, top companies that have formalized paying for top performance carve out additional salary increases (*e.g.*, an additional 3–10 percent) for star performance. The wide range of salary increases allow managers to have flexibility in rewarding and further motivating star performance. In fact, many top companies institute a compensation philosophy that reward top performers by paying base salaries comparable to the 75th to 90th percentiles of market competitive data, while average performers are compensated at or below the 50th percentile.

BEST PRACTICE

Rewarding top performers

Company name:	**ABC Corporation**

Problem faced by company:	ABC Corporation was in a habit of paying all employees across the board increases. During the weak economy and tightened budgets, the company found itself with reduced salary increase budgets and inequities. Some divisions with larger budgets paid out increases while other smaller divisions instituted salary freezes. The company had no formal salary administration plan or merit program in place to ensure that increases were given not on a divisional budget basis but on a performance basis.
Compensation solutions:	Especially during a down market, companies should take care to ensure that limited payroll dollars are distributed in a way to reward top performers.

A performance evaluation plan was set into place to objectively measure each individual's performance throughout the company's fiscal year. Once the performance evaluations were administered, increases were provided to qualified employees directly tied to performance. The company can reward high achievers with a greater increase than average performers. |
| Benefit to company: | By implementing a performance based merit plan, ABC Corporation was able to target its limited payroll merit budget more effectively and increase production among its employees. |

ANNUAL INCENTIVES

Annual incentives are one of the most commonly utilized pay-for-performance methods. While the actual design and delivery of annual incentives are as varying as the business strategies they support, there are some recurring concepts that appear to reinforce sound "reward the best, push the rest" practices.

Providing additional pay for additional contributions is a key concept. In short, if the payout line were plotted on a graph in relation to performance, the best companies tend to draw out an exponential curve as opposed to a straight line. For example, the greater the performance achieved above a targeted goal, the exponentially greater the payout. Therefore, top performers are motivated beyond just a one-to-one incremental payout relationship performance. Consequently, below average performers are equally penalized for not accomplishing established goals.

Top companies are increasingly providing annual incentive targets above market midpoints. For example, leading edge companies' compensation philosophies are increasingly focusing on annual and long-term incentive opportunities whereby base salaries are targeted at 85–90 percent of market midpoint, and annual incentive opportunities are targeted at 110–120 percent of market midpoint.

Top companies are also increasingly mastering the difficult task of aligning goal setting with corporate objectives. In fact, some companies are starting to bake into their performance plans and payout systems how employees perform given changing business conditions: a very difficult economy, adverse legislative impacts, or even windfall events that were unaccounted for during the goal setting process.

Long-term Incentives

Long-term incentives can provide significant wealth creation opportunity for top performers, and companies have historically recognized the tremendous attractive, retentive, and motivational impacts of these awards. In fact, long-term incentives such as stock options, restricted stock, and phantom stock have historically been a preferred method for employers to attract the best talent possible. Beyond long-term incentive awards upon hire, top companies also grant varying amounts of long-term awards as a means to reward star performance, retain star performance, and send a message to all others that there is significant wealth creation opportunities if given performance levels are achieved.

Best Practice

Companies such as Microsoft have already turned to restricted stock and performance shares as a key vehicle outside of stock options to reward star performers.

No matter what the method for delivery, rewarding the best while pushing the rest sends three very effective messages to all employees, including:

1. Employees can and will be rewarded for significant contributions to the company.
2. The company will hold employees accountable for their collective and individual performances.

3. The company will share rewards equal to returns provided to shareholders, emphasizing that employees are just as important as the constituents they serve.

In fact, research indicates that additional compensation, or lack thereof, as it relates to individual performance sends a stronger message to the employee than anything else ever communicated. Organizations have slowly come to realize that, to be competitive in an up or down market, they can't afford *not* to reward the best. Without an appropriate rewards system, the best, brightest, and most ambitious people will feel undervalued and ultimately leave for greener pastures—or, equally as bad, stay at their company and slip into mediocrity.

POTENTIAL PITFALLS

The "reward the best, push the rest" strategy can be very effective in creating a successful organization. The strategy, however, is not without potential trouble spots. The implementation of this type of system requires the design personnel to be cognizant of issues that could reduce the effectiveness of its use.

METRICS

Measurement is perhaps the most important factor in the success of any rewards system. Any system must be objective in order to be effective. As in prior discussions about variable pay, measurements must be carefully selected to insure the proper behavior. The measurement system must be well communicated.

The rewards system must be objective in design. Performance metrics should be well established prior to related pay increases, bonuses, or other rewards. The entrance of subjectivity into the rewards criteria creates a sense of unfairness among the employees. Subjectivity can also create a culture of "yes" people as everyone attempts to earn favor. Not only do other employees become resentful of "pet" employees, but the culture of creativity and challenging of ideas can disappear.

Discussion among employees about how much their peers are receiving should be monitored. Comparisons will occur despite attempts by the management to quell such conversation. Talk about relative rewards can be both good and bad. In some cases, it may be a motivation factor for those who are not receiving as much. At other times, this discussion can work to demoralize and segregate employees. A wider gap between the "haves" and the "have nots" requires more discretion on the part of the "haves."

This gap between haves and have-nots can also lead to other problems inside the company. Teamwork may deteriorate as a result of jealousy. Internal conflict must be monitored to prevent major issues due to cultural dysfunction.

Another potential issue in using this system is the problem of star or near-star employees falling through the cracks. Not all people are motivated in the same manner, so some top employees may not be rewarded in ways that actually motivate them. Also, some employees may fall victim to political or personal dislikes.

Rewarding only the best may also cause another pitfall. The rest of the company may sink completely into the morass of mediocrity as a result of apathy among the tier of workers who are not being rewarded. This situation is almost as dangerous as losing star performers because stars lose their support systems.

The economy itself is an issue. In a down economy, rewarding star performers may seem more difficult. However, continuing to provide a tangible reward for star performers is critical as they provide much of the competitive advantage.

Finally, if the company does not follow through with promised rewards, employees are likely to find a new employer.

WHAT ABOUT "RANK AND YANK"?

"Rank and yank" is the nickname for a process in which companies rank employees from best to worst and use the rankings to establish pay and employment status. Typically, the bottom group in this process is told to pack their things. Reallocation of compensatory packages may occur among those who remain.

THE PROBLEMS WITH FORCED RANKING

Forced ranking is the performance management process where everyone in a company, division, or department is ranked from best to worst in an effort to determine how to allocate pay and/or the implementation of a reduction of force. It is easy to rationalize forced ranking when the economy is down, when your industry is hurting, or when the company has a bad year. However, when a company forecast is brighter, it begs the question of why there would be a process for "admitting" some of the employees are less than satisfactory. A better attack would be to hire only top performers and eliminate the need to ever "force rank."

Merit-based pay is designed to pay employees different rates for various levels of competence and performance. The underlying criteria of a merit pay system can be summarized as (1) the employee's performance in relation to pre-established job responsibilities and expectations and (2) the employer's financial ability to pay.

In the 1980s, it was easier to differentiate performance when merit budgets averaged 8-10 percent. The next decade saw the merit budgets erode significantly, making it more difficult for companies to distinguish exceptional work using performance-based merit increases. When this occurs, it is difficult to truly link performance to bottom-line improvements.

Forced ranking can sometimes encourage average or mediocre performance. At evaluation time, half of the workforce may be force-ranked as average, while remaining employees will be ranked below and above this standard. To stay on track with merit budget, employers who force-rank generally align employees in accordance with the pre-assigned performance distribution percentages. This scenario results in intense internal conflict and can destroy team-work and cooperation. Employees who improve will squeeze their co-workers down a notch, in this scenario.

Forced ranking forces evaluators to make determinations on a person-vs-person basis. This also could cause management to move away from focusing on pre-established and objective job standards and toward making evaluations based on personal attributes. A "Pandora's Box" subsequently opens to all sorts of problems, including bias, corporate infighting, and even lawsuits – all demotivating factors that negatively impact the performance of the organization.

At the best-practice (anti yank-and-rank) example, the legendary CEOs of Southwest Airlines proposed from the outset to hire the very best and to train all hires to the fullest extent possible. By hiring on the right side of the curve, there is never a need to force rank. This culture has resulted in workforces that are motivated to perform at higher levels than most other employers. As opposed to "rank and yank," these CEOs appear to "bank" on hiring the right employees. Hiring and retaining the right, quality people is much more efficient than hiring a large quantity of staff to be laid off in slow times based on ranking systems.

Best Practice

As of 2002, approximately 20 percent of U.S. companies such as Microsoft, Ford, General Electric, and Cisco used this system. Typically, these companies use the "social Darwinism" to create a culture of high achievement. This up-or-out system is much easier to rationalize in today's faltering economy.

This process is rather callous in execution. By the very nature of the rankings it can be political and subjective in nature. Evaluations are person-by-person affairs, often without established performance standards. The competitive nature of the rankings is caused by the termination of the bottom tier, regardless of the actual performance level. The constant pressure to outperform the other employees causes internal conflict and erodes teamwork.

The rank-and-yank system potentially can be damaging to companies due to the stress it injects into the culture. The stress is even greater when those that remain do not receive the rewards of the recent past. Merit pay has historically been 8–10 percent of base salary, but it has been reduced to 3–4 percent in the more recent economic climate. The answer may be to hire only the top level performers and to avoid the use of rank and yank.

"Reward the best, push the rest" is a cutting-edge practice that may be a double-edge sword. If done correctly, star performers are attracted, motivated, and retained to the highest degree. However, if company objectives are not clearly stated, communicated, and tied to performance measurement, then companies can potentially be rewarding the wrong things that could ultimately destroy a corporate culture. The events leading to Enron's bankruptcy serve as a reminder of this possibility.

"Reward the best, push the rest" should not be a reactionary pay strategy because of a poor market. Instead, it should be part of a well-thought out, well-designed compensation philosophy that directly links to the goals and objectives of the company by heavily incorporating performance management.

CHAPTER EIGHT

TAKING CARE OF THE EXECUTIVE TEAM

OBJECTIVE

The concepts, ideas, and trends discussed previously help to shape well-designed compensation strategies. Much of the focus has been on the appropriate use of variable pay and long-term incentives, along with other nonfinancial compensation. These strategies can be applied across all levels of employees within an organization. However, special consideration should be taken when designing executive compensation programs. These programs need to be differentiated like the compensation plans for the best employees, only more so.

KEY POINTS

◊ The leaders of an enterprise are attracted, retained, and motivated differently than other employees.

◊ Financial incentives are not as effective unless the incentives are large enough to actually make a noticeable impact on the financial situation of the executive.

◊ Use compensation elements that reinforce the self-worth of executives.

◊ Compensation packages should positively align the goals of executives with the goals and culture of the company.

WHAT WE KNOW ABOUT COMPENSATION SYSTEMS SO FAR

The importance of compensation in the success of a business has been well documented. Compensation is perhaps even more instrumental in building a successful executive team.

The total compensation package is used to tune into the needs and desires of the employees in order to best attract, retain, and motivate them. The total package includes base salary, variable pay, and other benefits and perquisites. Over time, the definition of compensation has grown to include all components of the total package.

Compensation is fluid because of various regulatory, demographic, market, and social changes. Current events have increased the importance of executive leadership due to various outside pressures, including shareholder scrutiny and the spotlight on ethical behavior. Customized compensation is rapidly becoming a prevalent trend in compensation because of the increasing diversity among executives.

Companies are evaluating corporate and compensation strategies for consistency to evolve that they will achieve the same goals. Where inconsistencies exist, plans are being revised to ensure a consistent message. Companies are also developing and using better measurements to ensure strategy alignment.

Not only should the compensation strategy align with the corporate strategy, but the compensation strategy should also embrace and support either the current corporate culture or a desired corporate culture. The corporate culture also determines the value of positions and people in order to better establish the compensation requirements and offerings.

Compensation also plays an important role in the attraction and retention of star performers—those employees who provide exceptional contributions toward the success of the company. Sometimes these major contributors are not only interested in the financial incentives found in the compensation package, they are also very interested in a few more subjective criteria such as work experience and corporate culture.

Compensation package design also plays an important part in managing the bottom line. The proper compensation structure can encourage the behaviors that improve the bottom line. Through compensation and culture, the personnel of a company can be shaped into a workforce that properly focuses on the success of the company. The key is to make sure the right behaviors are rewarded.

The best should earn the most because they are the ones who have the biggest impact on the company. Other employees should be pushed to perform like the best or to support the best. It is also important to manage the differences between the best and the rest in order to prevent organizational discord.

THE IMPORTANCE OF COMMUNICATION

Communication is the key to connecting the compensation strategy to corporate vision. It's possibly the most important aspect of any compensation strategy. Communication breakdowns can be costly — particularly at the executive level where understanding and motivation are essential to personal and professional success. No longer viewed as an expendable overhead cost, effective communication plays a vital and measurable role in an organization's financial performance. Whether the communication challenge is one-to-one or one-to-many, effective communication is a tool to:

- Drive business performance and bottom line results
- Save money
- Promote understanding
- Clarify expectation.

Communicating total rewards expectations and payoffs to senior executives should be a critical part of the HR function. Messages need to be clear, personalized when possible, frequent, and detailed enough to inform executives about "what they have" or "can have" with various levels of performance.

EXECUTIVE COMPENSATION PACKAGES

The definition of executive varies from company-to-company. Typically, executives are identified by:

- Salary, salary grade, or title
- Status as a corporate officer
- Designation as an "insider" by SEC standards
- Significant impact on results of the entire corporation, or
- Inclusion in both annual and long-term incentive pay plans.

Executives are compensated differently because they have different responsibilities than the rest of the company. Effective executives are expected to be the strategic leaders of the company.

With leadership comes greater responsibility—executives typically construct operating and strategic policy for the enterprise—and the expectation of greater rewards.

The leaders of an enterprise are attracted, retained, and motivated differently than other employees for several reasons. These reasons include:

- Previous financial situation
- Self-concept (ego)
- Leadership skills, and
- Experience.

Previous financial situation. Many executives have amassed enough wealth to be more selective in their employment. The financial incentives are not as effective unless the incentives are large enough to actually make a noticeable impact on the financial situation of the executive. Therefore, it is important to find other elements to work in conjunction with a fairly large financial package. These may be in the form of perquisites or other work experience-related factors.

Self-concept. Part of the skill set that makes executives successful is their personal self-concept. Companies should use this as a lever by using compensation elements that reinforce the self-worth of executives. Caution should be used when boosting the self-concept of executives because it can become an inadvertent tool for the destruction of the company. For example, the ego of an executive may become so large that he or she starts to make unethical decisions for the company.

Leadership skills. Leadership skills are the most important piece of the executive skill set. This is also what differentiates effective executives from the general populace.

Experience. The demand for experienced top executives is greater than the supply, so the marketplace belongs to the "sellers."

TYPES OF EXECUTIVE COMPENSATION

An important factor in attracting and retaining quality executives is the company's compensation program. While base salary is of great importance, executive incentives, stock options, stock bonuses, and special plans for deferring compensation are equally important.

Although qualified pension and profit-sharing plans are "executive compensation plans" to the extent that executives are covered, the fact that these plans must not discriminate in favor of highly compensated employees prevents their use in providing special incentives for management. For this reason, many special devices have been developed to compensate the executive.

There are four major types of executive compensation:

- Direct compensation
- Noncash fringe benefits
- Deferred compensation plans
- Retirement plans

The basic differences among these four types and the differing concepts upon which they are based are explained in the checklist below.

- **Direct compensation.** As the term implies, direct compensation consists of immediate pay to executives in the form of salary, cash bonuses, and qualified stock bonus plans. Direct compensation differs from fringe benefits in that it typically involves cash payments or other evidences of indebtedness to the executive that can be readily negotiated or sold for cash. Direct compensation also differs from deferred compensation and retirement plans in that its tax impact is immediate (or occurs within a year's time) rather than delayed until some future date.

- **Noncash fringe benefits or perquisites.** Conceptually, perquisites or "perks" are those benefits that most employees think of as being fringe benefits. Thus, the perks that an employer may provide to its employees consist of noncash benefits such as company cars, workout rooms, and employee cafeterias

  In the context of executive compensation, however, directors, officers, and managers have come to expect perks "above and beyond" those available to the average employee. Therefore, many companies have developed executive perks that consist of such "extra" benefits as chauffeured limousine services, use of corporate stadium skyboxes, and expenses-paid attendance at trade or professional conventions.

  Perks tend to differ from direct compensation in that they typically involve the use of employer-provided facilities or reimbursement of expenses, rather than the payment of cash or its equivalent. Like direct compensation and unlike deferred compensation and retirement benefits, perks provide an immediate economic and financial benefit to participating employees.

Of the four types of executive compensation, perks have been most severely affected by changes in the tax law. Basically, the Internal Revenue Code now provides that all perks are taxable as wages to participating employees unless the perk is specifically exempted from taxation. In addition, Congress has expressed an interest in further narrowing the list of perks that are exempted from taxation (e.g., health insurance premiums).

- **Deferred compensation plans.** Deferred compensation refers to what would otherwise be direct compensation or a perk (i.e., fringe benefit), except that it is structured to postpone receipt of a portion of an executive's taxable compensation until sometime after it has been earned by the executive. In the context of this discussion, deferred compensation plans are a type of intermediate benefit located midway between the immediate benefits bestowed on an executive by perks and the long-range benefits bestowed under a retirement plan.

A common aim of a deferred compensation plan is to shift otherwise taxable compensation into a future year and, thus, defer, if not reduce, the income tax that would otherwise be paid to the IRS. For example, the deferral of income may be for a fixed period of time or until the executive has satisfied obligations to the company.

Types of deferred compensation include deferred bonuses, stock options, and the so-called golden parachute payments.

- **Retirement plans.** The term "retirement plan" refers to deferred compensation that takes the form of an employer-sponsored plan or program that accumulates funds that will be paid to participating employees at some future date, primarily upon retirement. Conceptually, retirement plans are also a type of perk or fringe benefit that provides benefits to participating employees at some distant future date. Perks, on the other hand, provide an immediate benefit.

Retirement plans take many forms (e.g., pension plans, profit-sharing plans, and simplified employee pension plans), and there is some latitude permitted as to the benefits that a retirement plan may provide to participating employees. Other than direct compensation, retirement plans are the most costly for employers to establish, maintain, and fund. However, retirement plans may be the most important benefit that employers can provide to their employees due to their long-range economic and financial effect on the well being of the employees.

Because retirement plans will lose favorable tax treatment if they do not meet nondiscrimination rules, few, if any, of these plans are designed to provide executives with special treatment or benefits.

BEST PRACTICE

Looking at the four major types of executive compensation, the typical pieces of the executive compensation package are:

- Base salary

- Short-term incentives (variable pay)

- Long-term incentives

- Benefits, and

- Perquisites.

BASE SALARY

For executives, base salary is less important. In part, this is true because those at higher organizational strata have different expectations of the compensation package. These individuals typically do not receive as much marginal benefit from an increase in base salary as those at lower pay scales. The primary reason for decrease in marginal benefit is the corresponding increase in income tax liability. Also, a highly paid executive is not as likely to receive as dramatic of an increase in lifestyle from an increase in base salary as someone who receives a lower wage.

Executives also have different expectations of the compensation package because they typically have a better understanding of all the pieces of the total compensation package.

SHORT-TERM INCENTIVES

Variable pay for executives is usually tied to division and/or corporate performance, rather than individual performance. Executives wield great power in setting the direction of their operating areas. Therefore, they must accept responsibility for the failures as well as the successes of their charges. As a result, variable pay for executives is typically substantial.

Like any form of variable pay, the structure, measurements, and rewards connected with executive short-term incentives should be well communicated to be most effective.

Variable pay accounts for as much of the total compensation for executives as base salary in most companies.

METRICS

Most of the metrics for variable pay awards are split based on the responsibilities of the executive. These metrics may range from financial measurements to measures of other things, such as patents, customer satisfaction, and development, depending on the company focus.

Goals are often set by means of a defined target. The actual amount of at-risk compensation is dependent on the risk aversion of the company. A company that is more willing to take risks will typically pay very well when performance is good and less well when performance is down. A low-risk company may not pay as well on the upside but will typically provide more consistency in salary and variable pay compensation.

LONG-TERM INCENTIVES

Long-term incentives form the greatest part of executive compensation packages. However, the usage of long-term incentives has become more complicated due to increased scrutiny caused by failures in corporate governance and economic turbulence.

Several methods of long-term incentives exist. Among the most common are:

- **Stock options**—the right to purchase stock at previously specified prices during a certain time frame after employment requirements are met.

- **Stock grants**—stock given to employees at no cost.
- **Restricted stock**—stock given to employees with the requirement to keep the stock for a given amount of time.
- **Shadow or phantom stock**—a stock-like device, which removes market effects, used to allow an employee to profit from stock performance without diluting the ownership of the company. Often, these are used by companies that are not publicly held.

Long-term incentives are one of the largest differentiators between executive and nonexecutive pay. Executives receive massive (when compared to others) amounts of long-term incentives. The primary reason for this is the responsibility executives have to promote the long-term success of the company. The incentives actually serve to further strengthen the fiduciary responsibilities of executives as agents for ownership.

BENEFITS

The benefits offered to executives are typically along the same lines as those offered to nonexecutive employees—medical, dental, vision, and life insurance. The primary difference may be the inclusion of more choices (in a cafeteria plan, for example) or more coverage paid for by the company. This extra coverage may include dependent health care coverage or specialized medical coverage.

PERQUISITES

Perks include such benefits as employer-provided cars, paid meals and lodging, use of eating and athletic facilities, paid entertainment expenses, participation in educational reimbursement plans, free parking, vacations, and more. The most common executive perks include company cars, larger or well-located offices, and financial planning consultation. Financial planning consultation is important because the wealth accumulated via long-term incentives and other investments often requires more attention than executives can afford to spare. These financial services may include estate planning, tax preparation, and investment planning.

Another important perquisite for executives is the supplemental executive retirement plan (SERP). These plans are used to provide retirement funding for people whose equivalent retirement plan would be greater than the current tax laws allow.

Other ways to attract, to retain, and to motivate executives fall outside of the auspices of these categories. Many of the other methods pander directly to the self-concept of executives. These may be:

- Challenge
- Visibility
- Prestige

Even for lower-level executives, these types of perks work because a particular position may be seen as a way to attain a position of even greater value to the individual.

TRENDS

Changing demographics and economic environments have made the challenges facing executives greater. Today's businesses require effective leadership for success. They can no longer ride the economic swell. This has increased the bargaining power of executives.

The recent economic growth caused an environment of "celebrity CEOs," who sometimes felt they were above the system. The faltering economy has changed this attitude. Widely reported scandals at companies such as Tyco, Enron, and WorldCom had negative effects on public and shareholder sentiment. This led to the beginning stage of restructuring executive compensation. Because of awareness about the potential for executive misconduct, compensation packages are now being designed so that the executive, acting in his or her own best interest, best benefits the company.

Currently, the debate over the use of stock options and other forms of equity compensation is changing the usage of long-term incentives. Although decreasing as a percentage of total compensation packages, long-term incentives still account for the majority of an executive's total compensation.

Mandatory stock option expensing and increased concern over dilution has decreased both the use and depth of stock option programs. Another cause for the reduction of stock option usage is the economy itself. Currently, over 90 percent of executives are dealing with some form of underwater options—options of no value.

Today, the best long-term incentive vehicles are those with a budgeted fixed charge to earnings. Restricted stock awards, which have been previously detailed, are increasingly filling the void.

As we learned in Chapter Two, companies are choosing restricted stock for the following reasons:

- Although restricted stock awards require immediate dilution of earnings per share (EPS), the dilution is set at the grant date and does not vary as restrictions lapse.
- The long-term nature of these restricted stock awards serves to align the goals of the executive with the long-term vision of the company.
- Restricted stock awards have an automatic value when granted, with restrictions on sale or transfer until restrictions lapse over time; therefore, the executive immediately owns the stock, has voting rights with the stock, and is eligible to receive dividends.
- Restricted stock awards have a high retention value due to forfeiture of the stock following an early departure.

In addition, a strong argument to diversify and utilize other key long-term incentives like stock-settled stock appreciation rights (SARs) and performance share plans can be made; but, each company is different and, therefore, each company will require careful attention to its culture and what programs will most effectively attract, retain, and motivate the key executive talent needed to succeed.

Elements of compensation other than long-term incentives are also being affected by the current economic situation. The most immediate impact is the more restrained upward movement in recent CEO salary levels. Base pay increased by only 2 percent and more companies decided against salary raises in 2004. Base pay and variable pay increases have been directly related to performance increases. In the long run, more increases should be in order as the economy recovers due to the leaning-down of most business operations.

Executive compensation remains a fluid study, pushed and prodded by the ever-changing regulatory, political, and economic issues. Fallout continues from recent corporate scandals. Nonetheless, there is a constant: Compensation packages should be designed to positively align the goals of the employees—including executive employees—with the goals and culture of the company.

INDEX